A Lady's Hair Is Her Glory

Understanding Power in Prayer through Obedience

All Scripture quotations are taken from the
King James Version of the Holy Bible.

A Lady's Hair Is Her Glory
Understanding Power in Prayer through Obedience
ISBN 978-0-9839526-8-8
Copyright © 2013 by Anita Joy Sargeant

www.apostolicwinds.com

Published by Inspire Media, LLC
www.inspiremediallc.com

Cover Design and Layout:
Angela Carrington

Printed in the United States of America. All rights reserved. No portion of this publication may be reproduced, or transmitted in any form or by any means, electronic, mechanical, photocopy, recording or otherwise, without the prior permission of the author. Brief quotations may be used in literary reviews.

A Lady's Hair Is Her *Glory*

Understanding Power in Prayer through Obedience

ANITA JOY SARGEANT

Contents

Acknowledgments		VI
Dedication		IX
Foreword - Rev. Lee Stoneking		XI
Preface		XIII

Notice the Glory — XX
1. The Glory of a Woman Is Her Hair — 1
2. The Glory of Young Men Is Their Strength — 11
3. The Glory of the Man Is the Woman — 19

Who is in Charge? — 38
4. The Head of Christ Is God — 39
5. The Head of the Man Is Christ — 47
6. The Head of the Woman Is the Man — 59
7. Angels Are Ministering Spirits — 73

Prayer and Hair — 96
8. Avoiding Shame and Dishonor — 97
9. Hair, Not a Veil or a Hat — 107
10. Is It Okay to Trim Our Hair? — 111
11. Nature Teaches Us — 117
12. The Spirit of Holiness (Includes article by Dr. James Hughes) — 121

History and Holiness — 134
13. Hair and History — 135
14. Set Apart for God — 163

ACKNOWLEDGEMENTS

Thanks to every holy lady in the family of God for understanding and adhering to the beauty of holiness. Thanks to all the godly men among us who admire and encourage ladies to be holy women of God. You are my heroes!

Thank you, Dustin and Amanda Wurst, for encouraging me to write when I didn't believe it was possible. You mean the world to me.

Thank you, Tim, Angela, and Shiloh of *Inspire Media* for your amazing talent and expertise. I thank God daily for all you have done and continue to do for this ministry.

Thank you, Brother Stoneking, for preaching and teaching on the power of prayer through obedience and its connection to a lady's uncut hair. Your anointing changed my life.

Thank you, dear Jesus, for being my Protector, my Counselor, my Friend, and my Father. I love You most of all!

How does my hair look?

"Sing, O barren, thou that didst not bear; break forth into singing, and cry aloud, thou that didst not travail with child: for more are the children of the desolate than the children of the married wife, saith the LORD" (Isaiah 54:1).

DEDICATION

I lovingly dedicate this volume to all of my spiritual children everywhere. I love you all!

Rev Lee Stoneking
—*Prophet, Evangelist, and Author with World-wide Ministry*

"I shall not die, but live, and declare the works of the LORD" (Psalm 118:17).

Foreword

It is most refreshing to read from the pen that has been dipped into the ink of life and then read the wisdom and power of a life lived in His footsteps!

Words painted upon the tapestry of our minds remain a treasure for life. Herein you will find such a tapestry making plain the simple and the profound truth of the Bible. You will glide smoothly through the pattern of revelation flowing from this author's soul and penned into the pages of your own life.

A LADY'S HAIR IS HER GLORY will become a study guide for your life and ministry to others.

My personal appreciation and thanks to author Anita Sargeant for making this work of truth and power available to one and all as we near the next greatest advent in human history—the coming of the Lord Jesus Christ!

—Rev Lee Stoneking

> *"Look where you are going, for you will go where you are looking."*

ANITA JOY SARGEANT

Jesus, I don't always understand Your ways, but I long to be close to You and will do all in my power to submit to Your will for the rest of my days. I want to see You someday soon!

Key Scripture:
"But if a woman have long hair, it is a glory to her: for her hair is given her for a covering" (1 Corinthians 11:15).

PREFACE

When Jesus' disciples implored Him, *"Lord, teach us to pray,"* He gave them an incredible prayer model we commonly refer to as "The Lord's Prayer." Before that model is effective we must first dedicate our lives to consistent prayer and then search the Scripture to eliminate any hindrances while doing everything possible to enhance every prayer we pray.

It is our privilege to submit to godly authority as it was ordained by God when He created man and woman, male and female. God made men very different from women and gave us little choice in those differences; however, God left one distinguishing physical feature in our hands to manage — our hair. His Word clearly expresses His desire for gender distinction in this aspect, but the choice to obey is ultimately ours.

God placed deep in the heart of a woman something that would help her make the choice to follow His plan — the glory of a woman is her hair. Even nature teaches us men should cut their hair regularly but women should allow their hair to grow long. The blessing given to us for following this simple command is powerful, anointed, and unhindered prayer. The curse for ignoring it is shame and dishonor.

King Solomon ultimately turned the hearts of the children of Israel away from God by loving strange women. The role men play in helping ladies maintain modesty and uncut hair is profound. Often the men of our day determine whether holiness is carefully adhered to or ignored. When men openly admire and honor holy, feminine women of God, the ladies feel loved and cherished and do their best to comply.

Strong male leadership that is founded in God's Word offers women security and strength. First Corinthians 11 deals with this subject. As we explore this passage, we understand the connection between gender distinction and submission to authority.

> *"Be ye followers of me, even as I also am of Christ. Now I praise you, brethren, that ye remember me in all things, and keep the ordinances, as I delivered them to you.*
>
> *But I would have you know, that the head of every man is Christ; and the head of the woman is the man; and the head of Christ is God.*
>
> *Every man praying or prophesying, having his head covered, dishonoureth his head. But every woman that prayeth or prophesieth with her head uncovered dishonoureth her head: for that is even all one as if she were shaven. For if the woman be not covered, let her also be shorn: but if it be a shame for a woman to be shorn or shaven, let her be covered. For a man indeed ought not to cover his head, forasmuch as he is the image and glory of God: but the woman is the glory of the man. For the man is not of*

the woman: but the woman of the man. Neither was the man created for the woman; but the woman for the man.

For this cause ought the woman to have power on her head because of the angels. Nevertheless neither is the man without the woman, neither the woman without the man, in the Lord. For as the woman is of the man, even so is the man also by the woman; but all things of God.

Judge in yourselves: is it comely that a woman pray unto God uncovered? Doth not even nature itself teach you, that, if a man have long hair, it is a shame unto him? But if a woman have long hair, it is a glory to her: for her hair is given her for a covering" (1 Corinthians 11:1-15).

Clearly, many modern cultures no longer hold to the value of gender distinction as found in the Word of God. Instead it is despised or considered old-fashioned and the principles of submission are often utterly ignored. It is more important than ever that the church in every culture carefully adheres to godly, biblical principles.

In this book we carefully look at the glory of a lady—her hair—and how that affects her relationships with both God and man. In the end analysis, gender distinction is important to us because it is important to God. As we study and allow His Word to lodge in our hearts, our relationships will grow and mature and His mind on the matter will become our own.

Gordon Sisters

Secret Place

In that secret place lost in Your embrace
How I love that secret place of prayer
In that secret place doubts just fade away
In that holy special secret place

Lord, I come on bended knee once again to Your throne
Asking strength from You in my time of need
And by faith I know answers I'll receive
In that secret place of prayer

All I need sometimes is a secret place to hide
When storms and trials mock my very soul
But I trust in God alone; He lifts me up on high
In that special secret place
In that holy special secret place

—Karla Gordon Trevino,
www.gordonsisters.com,
Secret Place CD

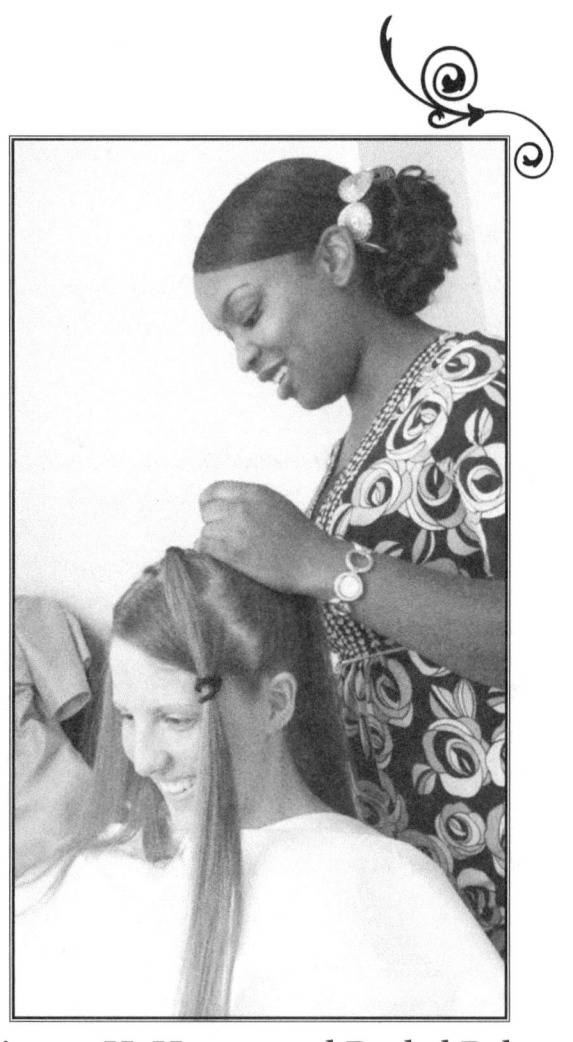

Brittany McMurray and Rachel Baker
on Brittany's wedding day

My Glory

I had the privilege of being raised in a strong Black community. My hairdressers taught me that to have healthy hair I had to clip my ends. Also, many times short hair styles have been "in." I didn't allow myself to align my hair with the teachings of the Pentecostal church where I was raised because I felt I was different from most of the other girls. My hair would never grow to my waist so I didn't have to worry about the whole "not cutting" thing.

I felt stubborn in several areas connected to gender distinction and particularly as it affected my hair. During high school God patiently and mercifully began to deal with me. Slowly my manner of dress changed along with my outlook on natural beauty, but I stubbornly held on to the myth that "we" had to cut our hair in order for it to be healthy and cute.

During my freshman year at Bible College I received the revelation on God's biblical standards concerning hair. I remember sitting in a class, listening to the teaching from God's Word and feeling vexed. "She has it all wrong. My hair is different from all of these 'others.' Her revelation is flawed! She doesn't understand my Black culture," I fumed. But as I considered the Word of God, I realized my thinking was flawed.

God began to reveal His plan to me. It was as if a light went on. My hair is my glory! There are angels connected to my uncut hair! My hair is my covering! The lights kept flashing. I walked away trying to deny what I was feeling but realized that a pair of scissors would never touch my hair again. As I looked around, I began to see other Black women just like me living for God with beautiful uncut hair. Since then I have never doubted once the importance of my glory. My hair continues to grow and God provides me with ideas and ways to fix it as I keep it right for His glory.

—*Rachel Baker*

Notice the *Glory*

- The Glory of a Woman Is Her Hair
- The Glory of Young Men Is Their Strength
- The Glory of the Man Is the Woman

CHAPTER 1

THE GLORY OF A WOMAN IS HER HAIR

"Her Hair Is Given Her for a Covering"

Her Hair is Part of Her Identity as a Woman

God placed something deep in the heart of a lady that glories or focuses on her hair. The glory of a woman is her hair. Many times when the long hair of a young girl is cut for the first time she will cry for no apparent reason.

There is something intriguing about the hair of a girl. It is part of who she is as a feminine and unique individual. When a girl cuts her hair it is different than when she changes into a new dress or coat. Her hair is her covering, a part of who she is as a lady and connected to her most important relationships—God and man.

> *"But if a woman have long hair, it is a glory to her: for her hair is given her for a covering"* (1 Corinthians 11:15).

The Little Girl Who Cut Her Own Hair

One day when Amy was only four years old she went into the bathroom taking the scissors with her, climbed up on a stool so she could see in the mirror, and grasping a handful of her hair she very purposefully cut a hunk of it off. The feeling that followed is one she will never forget.

She suddenly felt so much guilt and shame that she could hardly bear it. She felt unprotected and alone. She did not hesitate even for a moment but dropped the scissors, ran to the door and into the other part of the house to find her mother. Her throat constricted as she grabbed her mother's dress, pulling on it to get her attention, and confessing with sincere repentance and consternation what she had done. "Mama, Mama, look! I cut my hair!" Tears filled her eyes and rolled down her cheeks.

As Amy pondered the incident through the years it strengthened her resolve never to allow that feeling to wash over her again. In some ways she felt glad for the experience because the action is one she has never been tempted to repeat.

If angels become involved with rejoicing when a sinner repents, it is probable they are negatively affected when a little girl like Amy cuts her hair in disobedience. It is also likely that these same angels rejoice when she repents of this disobedience.

> *"Likewise, I say unto you, there is joy in the presence of the angels of God over one sinner that repenteth" (Luke 15:10).*

A Lady Focuses on Her Hair

Ladies are generally very conscious of what their hair looks like. They seldom lose focus of that. If one takes notice of women in a windstorm or a rainstorm, their biggest worry is about the effects of the storm on their hair. One may hear the despairing cry, *"Oh no! My hair!"* A lady's focus and attention are repeatedly redirected to her hair throughout each and every day. She likes it that way because her hair is her glory.

A Lady's Hair and Her Relationship with Men

It almost always brings a smile to the lips of a girl if someone says to her, *"Your hair looks nice!"* She loves the praise.

When a lady who desires to attract a man gets ready for a date, she gives careful attention to her hair. Instinctively she knows that long, flowing hair or attractively arranged hair will catch his eye and turn his head.

Hollywood is well aware of this. Many films that depict a woman reaching for the attention of a man will feature a lady with long flowing hair.

A Lady's Hair and Her Relationship with God

God takes note when a woman remains feminine and keeps the ordinance of uncut hair. He honors her by bringing the glory of His presence down upon her when she prays.

In the Old Testament, when the priests obediently washed themselves before going into the Tabernacle, the glory of the Lord would come down and fill the Tabernacle in such a miraculous manner that even Moses could not enter in.

> *"When they went into the tent of the congregation, and when they came near unto the altar, they washed; as the LORD commanded Moses. And he reared up the court round about the tabernacle and the altar, and set up the hanging of the court gate. So Moses finished the work. Then a cloud covered the tent of the congregation, and the glory of the LORD filled the tabernacle. And Moses was not able to enter into the tent of the congregation, because the cloud abode thereon, and the glory of the LORD filled the tabernacle" (Exodus 40:32-35).*

When we enter into that secret place of prayer with our hearts set on obeying His simple commands, He rewards our obedience with the glory of His presence.

His Face Shines through Her Face

The Lord beautifies the meek with His glorious salvation and His face shines through their countenance adding beauty that is otherwise unattainable.

> *"For the LORD taketh pleasure in his people: he will beautify the meek with salvation" (Psalm 149:4).*

The best asset of a lady who desires to be beautiful is her careful adherence to God's principles. The beauty that holiness adds is more precious than any beauty aid available.

> *"Give unto the LORD the glory due unto his name; worship the LORD in the beauty of holiness" (Psalm 29:2).*

So along with the prayers of the psalmist we ask God to make us beautiful with *His* beauty—to allow His face to shine through ours. It is a secret revealed only to the righteous.

> *"Make thy face to shine upon thy servant; and teach me thy statutes" (Psalm 119:135).*

Points to Ponder

- A woman's long, uncut hair is her glory and is part of her identity as a lady.
- A lady seldom loses focus of her hair. She is constantly aware of how it looks.
- Ladies often use their hair to help them attract the attention of men.
- God notices when a woman does not cut her hair and rewards her with answered prayers and the glory of His power and presence.
- When a woman embraces holiness it adds beauty to her countenance. His face shines on her face!
- The Lord beautifies the meek with salvation.
- Holiness is beautiful.

Prayers

- Jesus, I am a man and I ask You to help me be the leader You expect me to be. I desire to encourage others to keep the simple, biblical ordinances regarding gender distinction and hair.
- Jesus, I am a lady and it is my desire to obey You by allowing my hair to grow long—uncut.
- Lord, sometimes it is difficult for me to find a hairstyle that I feel good about. Would You help me?
- Thank You for hearing and answering my prayers! It is a privilege to be a holy woman of God.
- Lord, would You make Your face to shine on mine? I want my countenance to be beautiful.
- Thank You for beautifying the meek with salvation.
- Jesus, I am excited about enjoying the beauty of holiness for the rest of my days.

A Lady's Hair Is My Testimony

After receiving the Holy Ghost at age twenty, my spiritual journey toward living a holy life began. It was all new to me as I was raised in a large Catholic family. Never before had I walked with more confidence or felt more like a lady. My hair at the time was very short. My older sister, a hair stylist by trade, had practiced on her many siblings. My hair had been every length, style, and color you could imagine. When I came to the Lord, I was working on a degree in stagecraft, which included exams about hair and makeup. I loved the look of "long hair" but did not think I could live with this standard. I enjoyed my modern styles too much.

I began to allow my hair to grow longer but continued to trim the ends. I did not yet understand the power of uncut hair. Those who taught me Bible studies explained the biblical doctrine of uncut hair but I still felt no personal conviction.

One day I prayed a prayer, "God, would You reveal it to me if a lady's uncut hair is really important to You?" Soon after, I dreamed about it. In my dream I accompanied the youth leader's wife to the hospital where a little girl lay dying. The doctors could do nothing. The youth leader's wife walked into the room and began to take her hair down. It nearly touched the floor. She stretched her hair across the girl's middle as she lay lifeless in the bed. She then claimed the power that was on her head as she claimed healing for the girl. When the prayer was over, the little girl's eyes fluttered open. She had been healed!

When I woke from the dream, I turned on the light and opened my Bible. I found verses of Scripture about a lady's uncut hair and wept with conviction. Since then I have not touched my hair with scissors. That day I made up my mind to obey the Scripture. As a result, I have felt that same power I dreamed about in times of storms and in times of joy. Holiness is truly a gift and I thank God for it.

—**Kristina Wilson**

Rev. Joel Andrus

CHAPTER 2

THE GLORY OF YOUNG MEN IS THEIR STRENGTH

"Her Hair Is Given Her for a Covering"

The glory of a woman is her hair. The glory of young men is their strength. The glory of man is the woman. God asked women to allow their hair to grow. He created them so that though many other things vie for their attention, they never allow their hair to completely disappear from their realm of focus. God asked men to lend their strength to women and created them so their strength is one of the most important parts of their focus. Though life brings many distractions, they seldom allow focus on their own strength to completely diminish. God also asked men to be the leader of the family and created them so that women are their focus as well.

This chapter deals with a man's focus on his strength. Understanding the roles of men and women helps bring clarity to the subject of gender distinction.

"The glory of young men is their strength" (Proverbs 20:29).

Men and boys are very aware of what they can and cannot do. They often think in terms of strength and weakness. Little boys may compete to see who can carry the largest piece of firewood or which one can load the wagon the highest and the best. Then they may join ranks to see how much they can accomplish together. It is fascinating to observe their ingenuity.

Feelings of Accomplishment and Self-Worth

When a young man struggles to accomplish a strength or endurance goal, his buddy will stand back and watch. After his friend accomplishes the task, the person watching will then slap him on the back and dole out the expected admiration. Admiration is crucial to the relationship. This feeling of accomplishment followed by admiration gives him a sense of worth and adds to his self-image. He is a man and *"has what it takes!"*

When a Man Needs Help, He Will Ask

At some point while working, a man may decide *(to his great disappointment)* that he is unable to succeed without the help of someone else. Only then will he ask for help directly. This is not done in a haphazard manner. He carefully looks over his options and specifically selects the best person to assist him. Only then is he open to receiving assistance.

The author of the world-renowned book, *Men Are from Mars, Women Are from Venus,* makes the following observation concerning men:

> *Martians pride themselves in doing things all by themselves. Autonomy is a symbol of efficiency, power and competence (John Gray, Men Are from Mars, Women Are from Venus [1992], p. 17).*

A Man's Strength and His Relationships

When a man desires to attract a woman, he will do all in his power to let her know how strong he is. It is common to see him *"show off"* by flexing his muscles or by other more subtle means. This is merely his way of attempting to gain admiration. He is flattered if she notices his strength.

Hollywood is well aware of this. Many films that depict a man reaching for the attention of a woman will feature a muscular man.

A Man's Strength and His God

Young men have strength to give that no other child of God has. When young, godly men use their strength to empower the church and to overcome the wicked one, revival fires burn.

> *"I have written unto you, young men, because ye are strong, and the word of God abideth in you, and ye have overcome the wicked one"* (1 John 2:14).

God entreats the mighty men to give their strength to Him—to give Him glory and strength. When men embrace godly principles and lead with righteous judgment in the home, in the church, and in the workplace by lending their strength, God honors them.

> *"Give unto the LORD, O ye mighty, give unto the LORD glory and strength" (Psalm 29:1).*

Points to Ponder

- The glory of women is their hair; the glory of young men is their strength; and the glory of the man is the woman.

- Men are strength oriented and derive satisfaction from feelings of accomplishment.

- Men ask for help when they need it. Only then are they open to receive assistance.

- Men are flattered if a lady that has his attention notices his strength.

- God notices the strength of young men and asks them to use it to strengthen and empower the church.

- God asks the mighty to give Him their glory and strength.

Prayers

- Jesus, thank You for giving men strength to lead.

- Lord, thank You for adding a feeling of satisfaction to the heart of man each time he accomplishes a goal that requires the use of his strength.

- I understand that because of this focus on strength, men ask for help when they need it and only then are they opened to receiving assistance. Would You please help me to remember this in all of my dealings with men or boys?

- Lord, would You help me to express my appreciation using appropriate words each time a man lends me his strength?

- Jesus, bless and lead each man that I know and help them to lend their strength to their families in their homes, to the saints in their churches, and to their God in prayer, worship, and evangelism.

- Lord, I am a man and my life is in Your hands. I will give my strength to Your cause for the rest of my days.

A Lady's Hair Is Her Glory

Kami-Ann Giwa-Agbomeirele

ANITA SARGEANT

My Hair Testimony

At sixteen years of age God began dealing with me about not cutting my hair. I had attended an Apostolic church for three years. I noticed many of the women had long hair and figured since my hair never seemed to grow past my shoulders I was not ever going to look like them. (Some African American girls are blessed with hair length, but many of us struggle to attain length.) I had grown frustrated with well-meaning saints who assumed I was new and in need of conversion simply because my hair was shorter than theirs.

I felt confused and somewhat apathetic until I listened to a preaching CD by Rev. Lee Stoneking. The revelation that my hair was my covering hit me squarely. I was brought up believing that I had to cover my head with a cloth of some kind in order for the Lord to hear my prayers. What liberty I felt when I understood that God gave me my hair as a natural covering. Additionally, I learned that "long" hair refers to "uncut" hair. This made sense to me because regardless of racial/ethnic implications, women's hair simply varies – thicker, thinner, longer, shorter, curly, straight, and so forth. God understood our hair when He created us. Therefore, although hair length may vary, having uncut hair is a universal that those who choose to can follow.

As an African American female, culture teaches us that accepting hair breakage and hair loss is a normative experience. We are taught that in order to have healthy hair we must clip our split ends. I challenged myself to find ways to care for my hair without having to clip my ends, refusing to believe that 1 Corinthians 11 did not apply to me because of my ethnic background. I learned that a woman's uncut hair gives her power with angels, and quite simply, I want all the power with God that I can obtain.

—*Kami-Ann Giwa-Agbomeirele*

A Lady's Hair Is Her Glory

Ehizele and Kami-Ann Giwa-Agbomeirele

She's mine! Isn't she beautiful?

CHAPTER 3

THE GLORY OF THE MAN IS THE WOMAN

"Her Hair Is Given Her for a Covering"

The glory of women is their hair. The glory of young men is their strength. The glory of man is the woman. God asked women to allow their hair to grow and created them so that their hair is their focus. God asked men to lend their strength to women and then created them so that their strength is their focus. God also asked men to be the leader of the family and created them so that women are their focus as well.

This chapter deals with the fact that the glory of man is the woman. By studying a man's God-given responsibility, we can better understand the woman's role. We will explore the male role and connect that to the lady's role as she responds correctly in a godly manner.

God's commandment for a lady to allow her hair to grow long is directly connected to gender distinction and her submissive role in the family.

Contrary to popular belief, submission is not a form of bondage. The command of submission is actually given to the entire church as we will explore more fully later in this book. The family unit works seamlessly when each person responds to their God-given role.

Desire Is Born

When God placed Adam in the garden and gave him the task of naming the animals, Adam noted that they all had mates but he remained alone. In that moment, desire was born in him for a companion of his own. He turned to God and asked, in essence, "*Where is my mate?*"

> *"And Adam gave names to all cattle, and to the fowl of the air, and to every beast of the field; but for Adam there was not found an help meet for him ... And Adam said, This is now bone of my bones, and flesh of my flesh: she shall be called Woman, because she was taken out of Man" (Genesis 2:20, 23).*

Strength and the Woman

Men have two focuses when it comes to glory—strength and the woman. The virtuous woman is fascinating to a man, especially if she maintains a certain aura of mystery. *Her approval, admiration, acceptance, appreciation, and trust are important to him.* Some females unknowingly bring pain to the males in their lives because they do not understand what is important to them.

When a wise woman learns that *approval, admiration, appreciation, and trust* are an important part of her relationships with the men around her, an amazing thing happens. His automatic response to her wisdom brings harmony and success to their relationship. A lady maintains success in achieving these goals particularly if she understands their value, nurtures the feminine part of her person, and understands the value of and submits to godly authority.

> *"For a man indeed ought not to cover his head, forasmuch as he is the image and glory of God: but the woman is the glory of the man"* (1 Corinthians 11:7).

When two young people of the opposite gender become attracted to one another, they immediately notice that they think differently. He is focused on his strength, ability, and accomplishments while she is focused on her sense of community and relationship.

As we explore these differences we learn that if we make a few word adjustments when asking for support it makes a big difference in the reception of the other party. The key to understanding lies in a working knowledge of the Scripture's meaning as it refers to glory, strength, and relationships.

Community and Relationship

A girl or a lady loves to feel a sense of community and relationship. If her girlfriends help her on a project without being asked, she feels loved.

All of the girls understand that it is more fun to work together than it is to work separately. She feels loved because her friends care enough to assist her even though she did not ask, especially if the task is difficult or requires endurance or strength. It never occurs to her that her boyfriend knows nothing about this way of thinking. Ironically, he feels unloved when a friend pitches in and helps with his project without being asked. If a friend will simply watch and admire, this will give him a feeling of accomplishment and success. He will feel loved.

"Would you?" or "Could You?"

Asking for support is always accomplished by first asking a question. Questions that begin with the words, *"Can you?"* or *"Could you?"* convey doubt that a person has the ability to do what is being asked. This is fine if the task is monumental. For example, *"Can you climb Mount Everest?"*

Questions that begin with the words *"Will you?"* or *"Would you?"* have an entirely different effect. They convey a request or need for assistance.

Because men are continually wondering if they *"have what it takes,"* it is often an insult to hear the *"Can you"* or *"Could you"* questions, especially if the task is quite menial. The *C* words question his ability and strength and may make him feel as though he does not *"have what it takes."* However, it is an honor to hear the *"Will you?"* or *"Would you?"* questions. The latter makes a man feel needed and trusted. It eliminates any demands by offering an option either to accept or reject the opportunity to assist. It is important to insert this element in all requests directed to men. If they feel as if they have *"no options,"* men likely will balk at giving their assistance. Often demands are entirely ignored. Let's look at an example.

Bill and Alice

Bill walks in the back door of the house after a long day at the office. He looks toward his beautiful wife, Alice, standing at the sink and hopes for a loving greeting. Instead he hears her say, "Can you take out the garbage? The bag is quite full. I have been working all day and have used it often."

Bill hears a demand and knows if he does not respond he will be in the doghouse. It is as if she believes he should have come home earlier just to make sure that the garbage was taken out at the right time. He feels blamed. "Of course I 'can' take it out," he tells himself. "So 'could' she." He wrestles with the demand trying his best to bring himself to a place where he does not feel unappreciated and blamed. "I can," he states in a flat tone that he hopes is not offensive. He walks into the other room reaching for a distraction from the unpleasant feeling and without even realizing it becomes involved in other things and forgets all about her question.

Alice continues fixing the evening meal and as she feels more and more ignored she begins to seethe with anger and mutters to herself. "Why can't he do one simple thing like taking out the garbage when I ask him? I told him the reasons why it is important to me. I tried to ask with a polite tone and even though I am tired and hungry myself, I tried to make it easy for him—he still had his shoes on so it was a good time for him to do it right then, when he walked in the door."

"Maybe he just doesn't love me anymore. I wonder ... He didn't say much after he came in. What is he doing now ...? The computer ... again?!"

By the time dinner is served the garbage is brimming with trash, she is angry, and he has forgotten about it completely. She glares at him across the table, but he doesn't notice until he reaches for her hand to say the blessing. She jerks away, bows her head, and folds her hands in her lap ...

Applying the principles of asking simply and directly, using the *W* word instead of the *C* word and then offering lots of appreciation once the task is completed is the key to receiving the support needed. Let's try again applying these simple differences and obtain a different, more pleasant result.

Bill and Alice Try Again

Bill walks in the back door of the house after a long day at the office. He looks toward his beautiful wife, Alice, hoping for a loving greeting. She turns, smiles into his eyes, dries her hands and immediately walks over to him to receive his kiss. "I am so glad you are home!" she says enthusiastically. Dinner will be ready soon. Would you take out the garbage for me?"

Bill feels great! His lovely wife is fixing a fine meal—boy is he hungry! And she is excited that he is home ... that is always a good feeling. Of course he will take out the garbage! That should earn him at least another of her wonderful kisses! "Sure, honey! I will take it out right now before I take these shoes off. It looks like you have been quite busy. It is really full."

He gives her a wink, and she pauses to give him a little kiss on the cheek with the words, "Thanks so much, love. It means so much to me. Thanks!"

Just as he hoped, when he walked in the back door after taking out the garbage Alice noticed and again expressed her appreciation. "Thanks, Bill. Thanks again!"

"You are most welcome! Is there anything else I can do?"

"No, I will have dinner on in a few minutes. I know you have worked hard today," Alice responds.

He finds that he is almost disappointed that she no longer needs him. "Well, if you think of something else, just let me know," he says before he turns to go into the other room.

"Thanks, Bill! You are such a wonderful husband. I love being married to you." He reaches again for one more kiss before leaving her alone to finish the meal.

Alice smiles and shakes her head as she turns back to the sink where she is preparing the salad. "Wow! God gave me the best husband in the world. He is amazing!" she says to herself as she quickly finishes the work.

When Bill and Alice sit down at the table together and look at one another, their eyes sparkle with feelings of love and appreciation. He reaches for her hand to say the blessing and she squeezes it an extra time before letting go.

He looks at her and with a slow wink and a smile they begin to enjoy the meal together.

The simple yet profound understanding of a male's view on the distinction between *can/could* and *will/would* dramatically alters the response a woman receives when making requests. Instead of feeling challenged or mistrusted, the men in her life feel admired and appreciated. Her ability to respond with gracious appreciation every time assistance is received greatly increases the likelihood that the man will help her in the future.

Stark Differences

Because of these stark differences—a man's focus on strength and accomplishments, and a woman's focus on relationships—men and women often misunderstand, become offended, and argue. If he is trying to accomplish a goal *(possibly to impress her or to get her attention)*, she will often begin helping him without even asking! She *thinks* he feels loved and cared for when she does this. She is willing to help, even if the task is difficult or she doesn't really want to, just because she longs to feel a sense of friendship and community in the relationship.

He is offended by her actions because how on earth can he impress her with his great strength and ability if she is helping him? All of the reasons and incentives for doing the job are suddenly either greatly diminished or gone completely. He may not only be offended but he may feel angry and unintentionally say something unkind.

When ladies keep this concept in mind, it helps them build meaningful relationships. They realize the need for requesting support in a trusting manner. They refrain from assisting men unless they are asked to do so. Let's look at an example:

Ed and Molly

Molly walks in after the church dinner and begins to help her special friend, Ed, as he loads the decorations in the box. She smiles at him expecting him to be pleased, but he glares at her.

Molly is hurt because just when she felt excited about enjoying a sense of relationship and community, for some unknown reason Ed is angry. If she is not mistaken that anger is directed at her! So confusing! Just a moment ago he was attentive and seemed to want her complete attention. Now he acts as though he is angry enough to leave. Why? She finds herself at a complete loss for words and tears spring into her eyes. "What just happened?" she asks herself.

Ed fumes under his breath and struggles to maintain his composure. "What's the deal? I thought she liked me. She must think I am some puny, little weakling that doesn't have the strength to do a thing! She doesn't even trust me to accomplish the simplest task!"

And so they glare at one another and continue to misunderstand their simple differences. Ed's supposition that she does not trust him is strengthened when Molly hesitantly says, "Can you carry this to the car?" and hands him a vase of flowers.

He fumes as he mutters to himself, "Can I? Of course I can! What do you think? Are you afraid to trust me to carry a simple vase of flowers to the car?" Once again his anger flares almost out of control. "Do you think I am such a clumsy ox that I would break the vase?" he mumbles.

Molly can't tell what he said but she sees him scowl and mutter under his breath and she snatches the vase from his hands. Her eyes fill with tears again, and this time she storms, "If you don't want to do it you don't have to! I can carry them! It is just that I have all these other things to carry also and I just thought that you could help! I see I was wrong! Have you ever heard of this thing called a gentleman?"

Now she is adding insult to injury! Not only is she challenging his strength and ability but she is challenging his character, motive, and training. "What next?" Ed shouts at her.

"I don't have to take this!" He turns, slams the door, and walks away.

Ed And Molly Try Again

Now let us go back through this scenario from the beginning and find out what went wrong. Perhaps Molly can do better if she understands their relational differences.

Molly walks up and sees Ed working to load the decorations in the box. She greets him warmly and notices him and what he is trying to do. "Hi, Ed! I see you are helping the decoration committee. How nice of you to do that!"

He smiles back feeling important and admired because she noticed. She continues to watch, eyes glowing with admiration and respect. He feels great!

Finally Ed finishes. She lets him know just how great she thinks he is for giving his strength to the task. "Ed, you are such a helpful, dedicated man of God. I admire you for that."

As they prepare to head to the car she smiles in a trusting manner and asks, "Would you carry this vase of flowers to the car?" She hesitates until he agrees.

He readily responds, "Sure, I will be glad to." Molly smiles into his eyes as she hands him the vase.

"Thank you so much!" she exclaims cheerfully.

Ed's head is held a little higher, his smile is a bit brighter, and with his free hand he reaches for Molly's hand. "This is a wonderful girl! She really admires me!" he says to himself with a satisfied grin. He looks toward her and she smiles into his eyes with that trusting, thankful look. "Wow! I picked a winner this time!" he muses. He feels confident that he is moving in the right direction and says to himself, "This is the kind of girl I want to spend the rest of my life with!"

As they approach the car Molly trusts him to settle the flowers carefully so they will not spill over. She does not offer to help him or give him advice unless he asks for it. If he does ask for advice, she keeps her opinions brief and adds her appreciation.

She hesitates until Ed is finished so he can open the door for her. By the time he gets into the car beside her, both feel great! Molly smiles and says, "Thanks for being such a gentleman. It really means a lot to me."

Ed sits up a little straighter in the seat and with head back he begins to accomplish the next goal—reaching their destination. Once again, he does not need or want her help unless he asks for it. He wants and needs her trust and admiration.

Molly, remembering her mother's training, sits back and enjoys the ride even when she **thinks** they are headed in the wrong direction. She remembers that many times men surprise ladies when they think the men do not know which way to go. She knows that if Ed wants her advice, he will ask. If he asks and she feels she knows the answer, she will keep her response brief. The worst thing that could happen is that it would take them a little longer to get there. Molly breathes deeply and says to herself, "Molly, relax. He knows what he is doing. He needs your trust."

Molly's focus on Ed's need to be trusted, noticed, and admired completely changed his reaction to her. He not only felt great because of it but she felt wonderful as well. Soon Ed became so attached to Molly that he made plans to propose and marry her. He felt that she understood him and he felt comfortable when he was around her. He could relax. Ed asked himself, "What is it that makes Molly so different than so many of the other girls?"

Learning to Adjust

Since men are motivated and empowered by feeling needed they love to answer in a positive manner when they are asked the *"Will you?"* or *"Would you?"* questions, unless the requests are made in a demanding manner with a list of reasons why they must say yes. At that point the request becomes a demand. Men do not respond to demands; they respond to requests.

When one lady speaks to another and uses the words *"Would you?"* or *"Could you?"* they mean exactly the same thing. A yes answer to either question means commitment to do the requested task. A yes answer has nothing to do with ability or strength. It is difficult for her to comprehend and remember that a man's yes answer to her *"Could you?"* request may *simply mean that he has the ability and strength to accomplish the task. It does not commit him to performing the task.*

Sensitivity to her feelings may prompt a man to realize she is mistakenly using the wrong terminology and to clarify her request by asking, "Did you mean to say '*Would* you take out the trash?'" Teaching her to ask in a trusting manner helps her learn that it makes a difference to him.

Often when ladies offend men, it is because they do not understand the amazing differences between them. It is important to remember that *men focus on two things – their strength and women's trust, approval, admiration, appreciation, and acceptance of him.*

Her approval of who he is helps to keep him from feeling as though he does not *"have what it takes."* Her acceptance is reserved for times when it is difficult to respond positively to a decision he makes. Her loving acceptance during those difficult moments makes a big difference to him and actually creates in him a desire to change it if he can think of a way to do so.

Understanding and responding to these simple concepts brings peace and joy to our friendships. Men feel honored and trusted and ladies feel cherished.

> *"Likewise, ye husbands, dwell with them according to knowledge, giving honour unto the wife, as unto the weaker vessel, and as being heirs together of the grace of life; that your prayers be not hindered"* (1 Peter 3:7).

This cherished feeling makes it easy for her to foster her feminine side. This includes diligent care of her long, uncut hair. Since the man values her femininity, her focus on that area of her life pleases him and helps to accomplish God's plans for their lives.

Unisex

The unisex concept that is paramount in our day is wreaking havoc with relationships. As mankind disregards differences and encourages competition between genders, often both are disheartened and unmotivated. Relationships become a burden instead of a joy; God's plan for mankind is thwarted.

The unisex movement has created sexual confusion and neurotic behavior. The following quote from the *Encyclopedia of Occultism and Parapsychology* emphasizes the effect of hair on the spirit world and the dangers of a unisex society.

> *Hair has had an occult significance since ancient times. It has been regarded as a source of strength. The association of hair with sexual features of the body has given it remarkable force, and distinctions between male and female hair have emphasized sexual attraction.*
>
> *The unisex fashions of the permissive society and rock groups have tended to create sexual confusion and neurotic behavior* (Encyclopedia of Occultism and Parapsychology, *p. 572)*.

A man feels proud to be associated with a lady who remembers that her long, uncut hair is her glory. Because she is the glory of man, she fixes it attractively, nurtures her feminine side, and learns the art of responding correctly to her male counterpart. She is his glory.

Points to Ponder

- When God created man and asked him to name the animals, Adam noticed that they all had mates but he remained alone. In that moment, desire for the woman was born.
- Men glory in their strength and in the woman.
- When ladies understand the focus men have on strength and on the woman and use their natural abilities to nurture their relationships with men, both men and women are rewarded with feelings of satisfaction.
- Men focus primarily on their strength and ability to accomplish goals while ladies focus primarily on community and relationship.
- Men desire approval, admiration, acceptance, appreciation, and trust.
- Asking for support in a trusting manner, using "Would you?" or "Will you?" questions brings harmony to relationships.
- Often ladies help one another without even being asked and many times without waiting for permission to do so. This assistance is accepted, admired, and sought after. It adds to their sense of community. "Could you?" or "Would you?" mean exactly the same thing to both of the ladies involved.
- Men do not help one another unless they are asked to do so. To do so would indicate a mistrust of the other man to do the project on his own.
- When ladies adjust by using correct terminology as they respect differences, their relationships become acceptable and rewarding.
- The unisex movement has added confusion and neurotic behavior to our society.
- When women nurture their feminine side and admire the masculinity of their male counterparts, men feel pride in their association with them. The woman is the glory of the man.

Prayers

- Thank You for sending strong, godly men into my life that live for and follow You.
- Jesus, would You give me strong leadership from men that love You and desire to be a part of Your perfect plan?
- Lord, would You help me to have right relationships in the following areas?

  o _____

  o _____

  o _____

  o _____

- Would You help me to remember to ask for support in a trusting manner using words that convey that trust?
- Jesus, would You help me to remember to adjust the ways in which I react in my friendships according to whether I am dealing with a lady or a man so that I will convey love to both?
- Lord, I am a lady and I want to do my best to nurture my feminine nature and be the best friend and companion to others that I can possibly be.
- Jesus, I am a man and I want to be the best leader, provider, and protector with godly principles that I can possibly be. Would You lead me and guide me?
- Lord, You have given me godly friends and companions and I feel so thankful and so blessed!

Who Is In Charge?

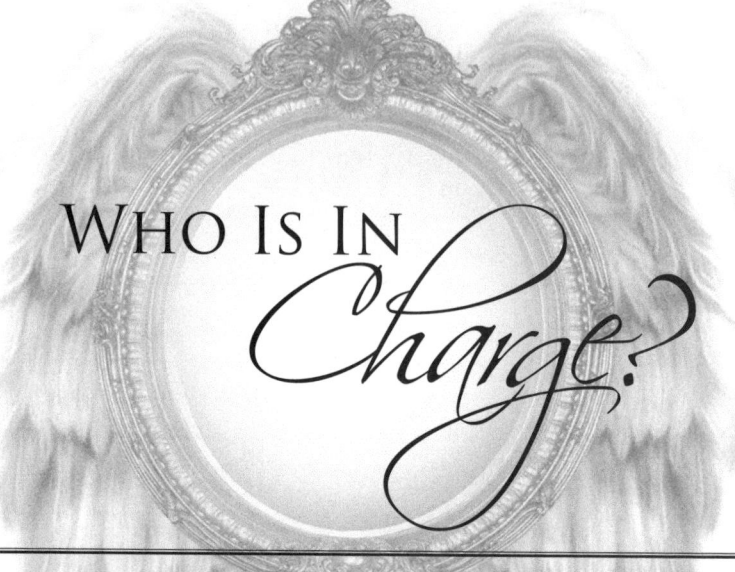

- The Head of Christ Is God
- The Head of the Man Is Christ
- The Head of the Woman Is the Man
- Angels Are Ministering Spirits

CHAPTER 4

THE HEAD OF CHRIST IS GOD

"Her Hair Is Given Her for a Covering"

The Order of Creation

In order to fully comprehend God's ordinance for a lady to allow her hair to grow long, we will first explore the order of creation.

The structure of authority in the church and in the home is not left to happenstance; it is ordered by God according to His creative purpose: God, Christ, man, woman, and angels. In this chapter we will explore the fact that the head of Christ is God.

"But I would have you know, that the head of every man is Christ; and the head of the woman is the man; and the head of Christ is God" (1 Corinthians 11:3).

Mary Submitted to the Virgin Birth

When the angel Gabriel visited Mary, the mother of Jesus, and told her of the coming child she would bear, she felt perplexed and asked, *"How can these things be?"* Gabriel reassured her that the child would be born before she consummated her marriage, while she was still a virgin. This child would have no earthly father but would be called the Son of God. Mary submitted to the plan of God leaving us an excellent example of submission.

> *"Then said Mary unto the angel, How shall this be, seeing I know not a man? And the angel answered and said unto her, The Holy Ghost shall come upon thee, and the power of the Highest shall overshadow thee: therefore also that holy thing which shall be born of thee shall be called the Son of God"* (Luke 1:34-35).

Jesus Submitted to His Parents and to the Cross

The Ruler of the universe humbled Himself and became a man. He was no less God for having done it but made Himself as one of us. He came as a servant to mankind.

> *"Who, being in the form of God, thought it not robbery to be equal with God: but made himself of no reputation, and took upon him the form of a servant, and was made in the likeness of men: and being found in fashion as a man, he humbled himself, and became obedient unto death, even the death of the cross"* (Philippians 2:6-8).

God became flesh so that He could dwell among us and be a part of the human family.

> *"And the Word was made flesh, and dwelt among us, (and we beheld his glory, the glory as of the only begotten of the Father,) full of grace and truth" (John 1:14).*

As Jesus grew He surrendered to the will of His parents as an example to us of the submission He expects as we adhere to His commandments, including the one that asks a lady to allow her hair to grow.

> *"And [Jesus] went down with [his parents], and came to Nazareth, and was subject unto them: but his mother kept all these sayings in her heart. And Jesus increased in wisdom and stature, and in favour with God and man" (Luke 2:51-52).*

Just before Jesus' accusers came to arrest Him in the *Garden of Gethsemane,* He took time to surrender His will to God in prayer. As a man His will had to be surrendered in order for the work of Calvary to be completed. As the church, we submit to the will of God so that the work of the ministry can be accomplished.

Though Jesus despised the shame of the cross, He endured by keeping His mind on the goal before Him—to offer the supreme sacrifice to free us from the bondage of sin.

When a lady understands that accomplishing the goal of allowing her hair to grow long results in effective and anointed prayer, it is a privilege and an honor for her to comply even when it seems difficult. Her submission sets the stage for a dynamic relationship with Almighty God.

> *"Looking unto Jesus the author and finisher of our faith; who for the joy that was set before him endured the cross, despising the shame, and is set down at the right hand of the throne of God. For consider him that endured such contradiction of sinners against himself, lest ye be wearied and faint in your minds" (Hebrews 12:2-3).*

Jesus Is the Almighty God

God gave all power in heaven and earth to Jesus Christ. He is the almighty God, the Everlasting Father, manifested in the flesh of Jesus Christ.

> *"And Jesus came and spake unto them, saying, All power is given unto me in heaven and in earth" (Matthew 28:18).*

Jesus Is the Visible Form of the Invisible God

When Jesus' disciples questioned Him about the Father, He replied, *"If You have seen me You have seen the Father."*

> *"Philip saith unto him, Lord, shew us the Father, and it sufficeth us. Jesus saith unto*

him, Have I been so long time with you, and yet hast thou not known me, Philip? he that hath seen me hath seen the Father; and how sayest thou then, Shew us the Father? Believest thou not that I am in the Father, and the Father in me? the words that I speak unto you I speak not of myself: but the Father that dwelleth in me, he doeth the works" (John 14:8-10).

The only bodily form of God is Jesus Christ. He is the visible form of the invisible God who created the heavens and the earth. The head of Christ is God.

"In whom we have redemption through his blood, even the forgiveness of sins: who is the image of the invisible God, the firstborn of every creature: for by him were all things created, that are in heaven, and that are in earth, visible and invisible, whether they be thrones, or dominions, or principalities, or powers: all things were created by him, and for him: and he is before all things, and by him all things consist" (Colossians 1:14-17).

Points to Ponder

- God predetermined a particular order of creation: God, Christ, man, woman, and angels.
- The angel Gabriel visited Mary and declared to her that she would be the mother of the Christ child.
- The Ruler of the universe became a man and dwelt among us.
- Jesus was both God and man.
- As Jesus grew, He submitted Himself to His parents and to the death of the cross just as we are asked to submit to God's holy ordinances, including those regarding hair.
- Jesus despised the shame of the cross but endured it because of the purpose involved—redemption for fallen man.
- Jesus is the almighty God and all power in heaven and in earth belongs to Him.
- Jesus is the visible form of the invisible God. The head of Christ is God.

Prayers

- Lord, the miracle of the virgin birth is incomprehensible to the carnal mind—the miracle of the ages! Oh how I love You!
- I wonder how Mary felt while she carried the Christ child. It must have been both wonderful beyond words and scary to the extreme.
- Sometimes I feel mixed emotions when You lead me down new paths that I don't understand. Would You help me to respond with faith as Mary did? Would You help me in these areas?

o _____

o _____

- God, thank You for becoming a man, living on earth, and dwelling among us.
- Jesus, You are both God and man. You understand human feelings. Thank You for giving to us in that manner. I love You!
- Lord, You became a man and were tempted in all points as we are but You did not sin. I believe Your power can and will keep me from sin as I surrender my life to You. Oh how I love You! Would You help me in these areas?

o _____

o _____

- Thank You for the example of submission You left for us. Thank You for being submissive to your parents and for being submissive to the death of the cross.
- Lord, I understand that the man Christ Jesus is the only visible form of the invisible God and that when I pray—Your name is Jesus.

A Lady's Hair Is Her Glory

Rev. Joel Andrus

CHAPTER 5

THE HEAD OF THE MAN IS CHRIST

"Her Hair Is Given Her for a Covering"

Once we have established that the head of Christ is God, we then begin to explore that the head of man is Christ. Submission to authority plays a part as we explore reasons for a lady's uncut hair.

God Gives Mankind Dominion

When God created the fowl, He spoke to the air. When God created the fish, He spoke to the sea. When He created the grass, herbs, and trees, He spoke to the earth. But when God created man, He spoke to Himself; He made man in His own image. Through this process He gave man dominion over all the earth.

> *"And God made the beast of the earth after his kind, and cattle after their kind, and every thing that creepeth upon the earth after his kind: and God saw that it was good. And God said, Let us make man in our image, after our*

> *likeness: and let them have dominion over the fish of the sea, and over the fowl of the air, and over the cattle, and over all the earth, and over every creeping thing that creepeth upon the earth. So God created man in his own image, in the image of God created he him; male and female created he them" (Genesis 1:25-27).*

God gave man intelligence to conquer all of nature. As man enjoys this power, it may be easy for him to forget that God *gave* him this dominion and feel as if he is equal to God. Any time man begins to think of himself in a manner that does not regard God as supreme, he is in trouble.

The reason the serpent was successful in deceiving Eve when he came to her in the *Garden of Eden* is because he tempted the part of her that longed to be like God. She was created in His image. Today, through the power of the Holy Ghost, we are empowered to be like God in a way that was not possible with the *Tree of Knowledge of Good and Evil* in the Garden.

A City and a Tower in Babel

Since the creation of man, he has struggled with submitting to God's authority. We find one of the earliest examples of this struggle in the story of the *Tower of Babel.* Men pooled their resources and began to build a city to gratify selfish motives. They had no desire to obey God's command to populate the entire earth but rather desired to make names for themselves using the dominion God had given them.

> *"And they said, Go to, let us build us a city and a tower, whose top may reach unto heaven; and let us make us a name, lest we be scattered abroad upon the face of the whole earth" (Genesis 11:4).*

God easily thwarted their efforts when He looked matters over concluding that their plans did not coincide with His own. He turned to the hosts of angels at His disposal and said in essence, *"Let's go down there and mix up their languages so they do not understand one another anymore. Then we will see how smart they think they are!"*

Can you imagine what it must have been like once the languages were confused? The workers could no longer work together because they did not understand one another. The initial shock, the confusion, and the ultimate parting of the ways undoubtedly brought some comic relief to the heavenly messengers involved.

> *"And the LORD came down to see the city and the tower, which the children of men builded. And the LORD said, Behold, the people is one, and they have all one language; and this they begin to do: and now nothing will be restrained from them, which they have imagined to do. Go to, let us go down, and there confound their language, that they may not understand one another's speech. So the LORD scattered them abroad from thence upon the face of all the earth: and they left off to build the city. Therefore is the name of it called Babel; because the LORD did*

there confound the language of all the earth: and from thence did the LORD scatter them abroad upon the face of all the earth" (Genesis 11:5-9).

God has the ability and used it in this case to change the way a person thinks, forms words, and communicates. Amazing! He is powerful and has authority over us even when we are completely unaware of it.

Submission to Civil Authorities

God expects us to submit to civil authorities. We should obey them in all matters that do not violate the conscience; however, it is never God's will for us to sin even if those in authority encourage or demand it.

"Submit yourselves to every ordinance of man for the Lord's sake: whether it be to the king, as supreme; or unto governors, as unto them that are sent by him for the punishment of evildoers, and for the praise of them that do well" (1 Peter 2:13-14).

Jesus, the Fish, and the Money

Jesus taught His disciples to submit to civil authorities and even performed a miracle to provide the tax money needed to comply.

"Notwithstanding, lest we should offend them, go thou to the sea, and cast an hook, and take up the fish that first cometh up; and when thou

hast opened his mouth, thou shalt find a piece of money: that take, and give unto them for me and thee" (Matthew 17:27).

The Safety of Submission

When we understand the beauty and the safety of submitting to and preferring one another, we find fulfillment and enjoy the blessings of Almighty God.

"Likewise, ye younger, submit yourselves unto the elder. Yea, all of you be subject one to another, and be clothed with humility: for God resisteth the proud, and giveth grace to the humble" (1 Peter 5:5).

Save Yourselves

It is the responsibility of every child of God to save themselves from the onslaught of the enemy by adhering to the gospel and following God's plan of redemption for mankind.

"Then Peter said unto them, Repent, and be baptized every one of you in the name of Jesus Christ for the remission of sins, and ye shall receive the gift of the Holy Ghost. For the promise is unto you, and to your children, and to all that are afar off, even as many as the Lord our God shall call. And with many other words did he testify and exhort, saying, Save yourselves from this untoward generation" (Acts 2:38-40).

The gospel message includes simple steps for redemption and then admonishes us to study godly principles that help us grow into mature Christians. Ultimately, responsibility for our salvation belongs to the person we see in the mirror each day. It is our responsibility to study the Word of God, understand what God expects, and obey.

> *"Wherefore, my beloved, as ye have always obeyed, not as in my presence only, but now much more in my absence, work out your own salvation with fear and trembling"* (Philippians 2:12).

Jesus Is the King of Kings

A person who sits on the throne is in charge. His/her directives and leadership are law; the subjects are expected to comply with their wishes. Jesus is the head of this spiritual family. He is the King of kings and the Lord of lords, and we as His children are princes and princesses. He sits on the throne of our lives because He is in charge.

Follow Me as I Follow Christ

As in any kingdom, authority is delegated in this spiritual kingdom. Paul revealed his understanding of this submission when he admonished the Corinthians to follow him as he followed Christ. He placed himself over them and then proceeded to give instruction that would help the Corinthians to understand the order of God's creation. When we understand gender distinction as God ordained it, His desire for a lady to leave her hair uncut and for men to regularly trim theirs makes complete sense.

> *"Be ye followers of me, even as I also am of Christ. Now I praise you, brethren, that ye remember me in all things, and keep the ordinances, as I delivered them to you" (1 Corinthians 11:1-2).*

Submission to God-ordained authority is a particularly valuable weapon against the enemy of our souls. As he seeks to snatch an unprotected individual away, God Himself intervenes.

When we submit to the orderly plan God lays out, we are safe from the enemies of the King, our Father, and live under the canopy of His protection. We feel confident of our God-given position in the family of God.

Submission to the Ministry

It is the will of God that believers benefit from anointed preaching and teaching. The key to growth and maturity is absorbing godly principles from the body of Christ and from our own personal study.

> *"For after that in the wisdom of God the world by wisdom knew not God, it pleased God by the foolishness of preaching to save them that believe" (1 Corinthians 1:21).*

Submitting to godly authority is a multifaceted event. As we obey them that have the rule over us, God holds them responsible for preaching and teaching the truth so that souls are not led astray. Ultimately, He holds us responsible to respond to the message preached.

The Ministry of Receiving

Prophet T. W. Barnes once taught the key element of an anointed service. He proposed that anointing comes when the Word goes out and is received by willing hearts. When the Word is preached but not received, the presence of God does not move. *Our response* to anointed teaching and preaching is just as important to the moving of the Spirit in our services as is the anointed ministry.

In the following verse it appears that the writer of Hebrews, feeling the responsibility for the care of the saints, reaches to the church for assistance. He asks if they would be willing to pray for leadership.

> *"But to do good and to communicate forget not: for with such sacrifices God is well pleased. Obey them that have the rule over you, and submit yourselves: for they watch for your souls, as they that must give account, that they may do it with joy, and not with grief: for that is unprofitable for you. Pray for us: for we trust we have a good conscience, in all things willing to live honestly" (Hebrews 13:16-18).*

The Five-fold Ministry

God has given us godly apostles, prophets, evangelists, pastors, and teachers to lead us spiritually. These offices and their functions are necessary for the church to grow and mature according to His plan and purpose.

> *"And he gave some, apostles; and some, prophets; and some, evangelists; and some, pastors and teachers; for the perfecting of the saints, for the work of the ministry, for the edifying of the body of Christ" (Ephesians 4:11-12).*

God gave each of these offices of the *five-fold ministry* different functions. To better understand this we quote from author Lee Stoneking:

> *These offices are listed in order of administration. Each one depends upon the previous office for its existence. The success of each office is dependent upon the healthy function and order of the other four offices:*
>
> - *Apostles — Govern*
> - *Prophets — Guide*
> - *Evangelists — Gather*
> - *Pastors — Guard*
> - *Teachers — Ground*
>
> (*Lee Stoneking,* Five-Fold Ministry and Spiritual Insights *[2003], pp. 29-30).*

When we submit to God's authority in our lives and allow the ministry to be guided by the power of the *five-fold ministry,* His will is accomplished. Remaining under the authority of Christ brings the power of God's blessings to rest upon us. The head of man is Christ.

Points to Ponder

- We are created by God in His image.
- God gave mankind dominion over all the earth.
- God judges men, like those who built the Tower of Babel, who put themselves in a position that does not honor God and His plan for man.
- There is safety in submission to authority.
- We are commanded to work out our own salvation with fear and trembling.
- The authority over us is delegated by God.
- God admonishes the ministry to take a certain amount of responsibility for the souls of those they minister to.
- The key to anointed services is for saints to receive the Word as it is taught or preached.
- The five-fold ministry is used to mature and perfect the saints. The head of man is Christ.

Prayers

- Thank You, God, for creating us in Your image.
- Lord, we appreciate and respect the dominion power You have given to us.
- Jesus, would You help me to keep a humble and contrite spirit?
- God, we understand that You have delegated authority and we are expected to submit. Would You help us in the following areas?

  o _____

  o _____

- God, I realize that the ministry has been charged with a certain amount of responsibility for my eternal soul. Would you bless them today and give them strength for the task?
- Jesus, it is my desire to become engaged in the ministry of receiving during every class, service, or other ministry point in my life so that Your power and strength will have free flow in my life.
- I love You and give You complete access and power in all areas of my life.

Rev. Tim and Angela Carrington

CHAPTER 6

THE HEAD OF THE WOMAN IS THE MAN

"Her Hair Is Given Her for a Covering"

Once we have established that the head of Christ is God and the head of man is Christ, we then begin to explore that the head of the woman is the man. Submission to authority, both in the church and in the home, plays a part as we explore the reasons why a lady does not cut her hair.

Adam Needed the Woman

God created woman as a *helper* or an aid for man. Man *needed* the woman. This praises a woman's strength and purpose rather than her subordination. Woman was created because man needed her strength, not because he needed a servant.

> *"And the LORD God said, It is not good that the man should be alone; I will make him an help meet for him" (Genesis 2:18).*

Adam Was Formed First, Then Eve

When God created the human species He formed Adam first and then Eve. It was part of His creative purpose for mankind from the beginning to position man as the head of the woman.

> *"And the rib, which the LORD God had taken from man, made he a woman, and brought her unto the man. And Adam said, This is now bone of my bones, and flesh of my flesh: she shall be called Woman, because she was taken out of Man. Therefore shall a man leave his father and his mother, and shall cleave unto his wife: and they shall be one flesh" (Genesis 2:22-24).*

God created Adam and gave him dominion over the land and animals. Later God created Eve from Adam's side. After the Fall, He gave Adam dominion over the woman as well.

> *"Unto the woman he said, I will greatly multiply thy sorrow and thy conception; in sorrow thou shalt bring forth children; and thy desire shall be to thy husband, and he shall rule over thee" (Genesis 3:16).*

From the time of the Fall in the Garden of Eden, God arranged that women would have a strong desire to please their husbands and that their husbands would rule over them.

This does not mean a lady's value, intelligence, or worth is less than a man's qualities. Paul clarified this by inserting the statement, *"Nevertheless neither is the man without the woman, neither the woman without the man, in the Lord" (1 Corinthians 11:11),* so that everyone understands that men and women are interdependent. They need one another to function effectively, especially in the kingdom of God. Neither gender is superior in the sight of God. Men and women are equal in rights but not equivalent in roles. They derive their value and uniqueness by submitting to Him and His plan.

Unconditional Love

The key to understanding God's plan lies in understanding the command for men to love their wives as Christ loved the church.

> *"Therefore as the church is subject unto Christ, so let the wives be to their own husbands in every thing. Husbands, love your wives, even as Christ also loved the church, and gave himself for it" (Ephesians 5:24-25).*

Christ loves *us* unconditionally. He loves us so much that when we deserved to be punished He took our place. A man who understands this concept will apply it to his relationships with his family and will protect and shield them even when he may feel they deserve less.

> *"For even the Son of man came not to be ministered unto, but to minister, and to give his life a ransom for many" (Mark 10:45).*

Scripture mandates that women submit and that men be the head of the family. When the wife offers her unconditional love or reverence *(in the form of approval, admiration, appreciation, and acceptance)* and the man cherishes and loves his wife with the same unconditional love that Christ uses to love the church, emotional needs are met and God's will for the family is accomplished.

> *"Nevertheless let every one of you in particular so love his wife even as himself; and the wife see that she reverence her husband" (Ephesians 5:33).*

God Created Us Male and Female

From the beginning God created man and woman to be quite different from one another. Author James Dobson makes the following comment regarding one of the remarkable differences in the creation of male and female:

> *It was perplexing for me to watch this notion called "unisex" gain acceptance ... Males and females also carry a different chromosome pattern in every cell of their bodies. How could boys and girls be identical if their DNA is different? (James Dobson,* Bringing up GIRLS *[2010], p. 26).*

Left Brain/Right Brain Differences

The brains of males and females are visibly different even before birth. To better understand this difference we will first explore the brain as it functions on both the right and left sides.

Wikipedia reports:

> *The human brain is divided into two hemispheres—left and right. Scientists continue to explore how some cognitive functions tend to be dominated by one side or the other, that is, how they are lateralized.* (Wikipedia, Lateralization of brain function.)

Dan Eden writes in his article *"Left Brain/Right Brain":*

> *Our brain, like the rest of our anatomy, is made up of two halves, a left brain and a right brain. There's a big fold that goes from front to back in our brain, essentially dividing it into two distinct and separate parts. Well, almost separate. They are connected to each other by a thick cable of nerves at the base of each brain. This sole link between the two giant processors is called the corpus callosum. Think of it as an Ethernet cable or network connection between two incredibly fast and immensely powerful computer processors, each running different programs from the same input* (Dan Eden, "Left Brain/Right Brain," www.viewzone2.com.)

According to Eden's article, the results of recent research show the following left brain/right brain differences:

LEFT BRAIN FUNCTIONS	RIGHT BRAIN FUNCTIONS
uses logic	uses feeling
detail oriented	"big picture" oriented
facts rule	imagination rules
words and language	symbols and images
present and past	present and future
math and science	philosophy & religion
can comprehend	can "get it" (i.e., meaning)
knowing	believing
acknowledges	appreciates
order/pattern	spatial perception
perception	knows object function
knows object name	fantasy based
reality based	presents possibilities
forms strategies	impetuous
practical	risk taking
safe	

There is a significant difference in how God formed the way left brain/right brain functions work depending on the gender of the child. A female fetus develops the right brain and the ability to switch back and forth between the two functions much more effectively than a male fetus.

The Word Aflame Publications Adult Teacher's Manual further explains the corpus callosum:

> *Medical science has discovered that the corpus callosum connects the right and left sides of*

the brain with more than 300 million fibers that function as cables to transmit impulses from one place to another. Before birth, the gush of testosterone in a male fetus generally dissolves portions of these fibers, decreasing their number. The opposite generally occurs in an unborn female. Estrogen causes the nerve cells to grow more of the connecting fibers and expand the corpus callosum. The difference in the size of the space between the right and left sides of the male and female brain is generally so pronounced it can be visually detected on an ultrasound of the fetus (Celebration Series, vol. 1, First Principles, Lesson 4, Male and Female [Fall 2010]).

God Created Us to Fulfill Specific Roles

Men maintain a leadership role that has nothing to do with value, importance, or intelligence but rather with God's simple order of creation. Man's creation empowers him for his God-given responsibility. The remarkable differences in the creation of man and woman are some of the most fascinating in the list of nature's phenomena. Lesson 4 of the 2010 Adult Teacher's Manual makes note of the following differences:

Men and women are different. Men are basically full of action while women are more concerned with emotional connections. Men speak the language of action while women speak the language of relationships. Men tend to externalize, and women tend to internalize.

Men generally find their identity in their work or job; women often find identity in their family and children. Men tend to compete; women generally cooperate. In navigating, women generally follow landmarks while men tend to see a geometric system of routes. While little boys often play with mechanical trucks and make noises, girls often play with dolls and make conversation. The list of comparisons could go on almost indefinitely (Celebration Series, vol. 1, First Principles, Lesson 4, Male and Female [Fall 2010]).

Men — Their Responsibility and Motivation

Men feel satisfaction and motivation when they succeed in fulfilling a need. God plants that satisfaction in their hearts as a reward for fulfilling their God-given role in the family.

Author John Gray, in his book *Men are from Mars, Women are from Venus,* observes that **men are *"motivated and empowered when they feel needed"*** (p. 43).

Men are designed physically to be the primary breadwinners for the family. They are generally built stronger and more muscular. They feel a sense of worth when they use that strength to successfully support and provide for their families.

> *"But if any provide not for his own, and specially for those of his own house, he hath denied the faith, and is worse than an infidel"* (1 Timothy 5:8).

Women — Their Responsibility and Motivation

A woman feels a sense of worth when she creates and maintains meaningful relationships. The relationships she creates and nourishes assist her in feeling cherished and motivate her to do more.

John Gray observes that ***women are "motivated and empowered when they feel cherished"*** *(Men Are from Mars, Women Are from Venus, p. 43).*

A lady's primary God-given role is to be the keeper of the home. Though she is often called upon to also be a breadwinner or to help with the monumental task of making a living, the most fulfilling role she plays is that of a homemaker.

God made women with this purpose in mind, creating them to bear the children, and adding many soft touches that help to make them excellent homemakers.

> *"To be discreet, chaste, keepers at home, good, obedient to their own husbands, that the word of God be not blasphemed" (Titus 2:5).*

Accepting God's Delegated Authority

Jesus, the King of kings, delegates authority to men and they take responsibility for their families. It is the man's responsibility to understand the woman well enough to give her honor and deference, to loan his strength when needed, and to provide for the family. This is so important that God says if they do not do this their prayers are hindered; in other words—if they don't take care of their delegated responsibilities, they are in trouble with their Boss.

> *"Likewise, ye husbands, dwell with them according to knowledge, giving honour unto the wife, as unto the weaker vessel, and as being heirs together of the grace of life; that your prayers be not hindered" (1 Peter 3:7).*

A man's role in leadership is enacted by worshiping the one true God, then protecting, providing, and empowering those under his authority. When a man rules using the model of Christ leading the church, those under his authority feel his consideration of their thoughts and feelings, his caring, his strength, and his protection.

> *"Husbands, love your wives, even as Christ also loved the church, and gave himself for it" (Ephesians 5:25).*

A woman's role is to worship the one true God and then submit to God-given authority. Her role of submission is not one of subordination as it is referred to by those who have suffered abuse from inconsiderate and selfish male authority. Godly submission is a *privilege* as it protects, gives direction, considers, and loves just as Christ loves the church and gave Himself for it.

"Wives, submit yourselves unto your own husbands, as it is fit in the Lord" (Colossians 3:18).

As men and women work together in these areas, angels are sent to minister to them. Our submission to God's order of creation makes it possible for our prayers to be effective.

If we try to approach the throne room of God without first positioning ourselves in this manner, our contact with Almighty God will be hindered if not severed. We cannot effectively pray while dishonoring the authority structure God has placed in our lives; however, when we position ourselves correctly we find a direct line to the throne of God.

Points to Ponder

- God arranged that women would have a strong desire to please their husbands and that their husbands would rule over them.
- Unconditional love is the key to successful family relationships and is commanded by God.
- When a woman fosters a spirit of acceptance, the men in her life feel a strong desire to offer her support.
- God created mankind, male and female with marked differences.
- God delegated our roles so that when they are fulfilled we find a feeling of satisfaction.
- Men are motivated and empowered when they feel needed.
- Women are motivated and empowered when they feel cherished.
- When we accept God's delegated authority in our lives we find peace in our relationships—with both God and man.

Prayers

- Jesus, as a lady it is my desire to please those men that are in authority over me and to maintain godly relationships. Would You give me wisdom and knowledge in those areas?
- Lord, thank You so much for Your unconditional love. I don't deserve it but I appreciate it so very much.
- I desire to love unconditionally as You do in all of my relationships. Would You help me?
- Jesus, I am a lady and desire to foster a spirit of acceptance.
- Lord, I am a man and desire to respect those whom You have put in my care. I feel the heaviness of this great responsibility. Would You anoint me to offer my support, strength, protection, leadership, and love?
- God, thank You for creating men and women so differently. I am glad that I am a lady/man.
- Jesus, I accept the place in the body of Christ where You have placed me and I will follow Your perfect will in connection with Your divine authority.

Watcher in the Night
Thomas Blackshear, Artist

CHAPTER 7

Angels Are Ministering Spirits

"Her Hair Is Given Her for a Covering"

Angelic Commands

Angelic commands come directly from God. Only through effective prayer can we engage in the power transmitted by angels. When a godly lady's hair is uncut she qualifies. When a godly man regularly trims his hair, he qualifies. She needs him to regularly trim his hair so that their lives will be blessed. He needs her to leave her hair uncut. It is a joint effort of simple obedience. This brings spiritual power and blessing to their relationship and their lives.

> *"For the man is not of the woman: but the woman of the man. Neither was the man created for the woman; but the woman for the man. For this cause ought the woman to have power on her head because of the angels" (1 Corinthians 11:8-10).*

Simple Obedience—the Key to Power

A spirit-filled, praying lady who makes the commitment to live by simple obedience to God's Word becomes a perfect channel for God to work through. He sends angels to conquer the enemy and gain victory over Satan. The power generated affects not only the lady but the whole church body.

Angels Minister to the Church

Angels are ministering spirits to the heirs of salvation—the church. God sends angels to help us in response to our prayers and our submission. God's angels are intertwined with all God accomplishes.

> *"Are they not all ministering spirits, sent forth to minister for them who shall be heirs of salvation?" (Hebrews 1:14)*

The Wonder of Angels

The references to multitudes of angels moving through the heavens paint a beautiful picture. We can almost hear their voices as multitudes proclaim the wonders of God.

> *"And I beheld, and I heard the voice of many angels round about the throne and the beasts and the elders: and the number of them was ten thousand times ten thousand, and thousands of thousands; saying with a loud voice, Worthy is the Lamb that was slain to receive power, and riches, and wisdom, and strength, and*

honour, and glory, and blessing" (Revelation 5:11-12).

The organization that must be in place for the multitudes of angels to accomplish the tasks that God asked them to do is quite a feat in itself. When we consider their swift movements and changes in appearance—all of this adds angelic mystique to the miraculous!

Innumerable Company of Angels

The writer of Hebrews refers to angels as *"an innumerable company."* God does not run out of resources as He ministers to our needs.

> *"But ye are come unto mount Sion, and unto the city of the living God, the heavenly Jerusalem, and to an innumerable company of angels" (Hebrews 12:22).*

Mighty Hosts of Angels

Scripture is filled with references, both direct and indirect, of angelic hosts who obey the commands of Almighty God on behalf of His people. Often we read the scriptural phrase *"Lord of hosts"* instead of just Lord. It appears that the writers are reminding us that God has a host of angels at His command at all times. There is absolutely nothing too hard for Him!

As we consider the mighty host of angels that God uses to fulfill His will our faith increases. Though we do not pray to or worship angels and most often do not see them, we do understand from Scripture their constant interaction in the lives of saints. God is able to do exceeding abundantly above all that we can imagine asking Him for. It is impossible to separate God from angels. They are actively involved in the affairs of men and women especially in response to sincere and earnest prayer.

> *"That Christ may dwell in your hearts by faith; that ye, being rooted and grounded in love, may be able to comprehend with all saints what is the breadth, and length, and depth, and height; and to know the love of Christ, which passeth knowledge, that ye might be filled with all the fulness of God. Now unto him that is able to do exceeding abundantly above all that we ask or think, according to the power that worketh in us" (Ephesians 3:17-20).*

His Throne in the Heavens

The Lord has a kingdom in the heavens where mighty angels worship Him and do His commandments. They are His ministers that seek to please Him and faithfully carry out His wishes.

> *"The LORD hath prepared his throne in the heavens; and his kingdom ruleth over all. Bless the LORD, ye his angels, that excel in strength, that do his commandments, hearkening unto the voice of his word. Bless ye the LORD, all ye his hosts; ye ministers of his, that do his pleasure" (Psalm 103:19-21).*

Angels Protect Us

Angels congregate when saints gather. They are not only near them but they *deliver* them! Angels stand with swords of flaming fire and fight against the enemies of the Lord. Satan is afraid of the saints of God, for he has more than just them to contend with. Saints of God have angels surrounding them and the baptism of the Holy Ghost within them. *They are not alone!*

> *"There shall no evil befall thee, neither shall any plague come nigh thy dwelling. For he shall give his angels charge over thee, to keep thee in all thy ways. They shall bear thee up in their hands, lest thou dash thy foot against a stone" (Psalm 91:10-12).*

Our Personal Angels Watch Over Us

When Jesus talked of His disciples becoming as little children, He referred to a little one's personal angels.

> *"Take heed that ye despise not one of these little ones; for I say unto you, That in heaven their angels do always behold the face of my Father which is in heaven" (Matthew 18:10).*

God's holy angels stay very close to and camp around those that fear God and keep His commandments. It is the saint's promise of divine intervention especially in time of need.

> *"The angel of the LORD encampeth round about them that fear him, and delivereth them"* *(Psalm 34:7)*

If we pray when someone attempts to destroy us, God will send our personal angels to take care of it; we will not have to lift a finger.

David's Personal Angel

David, in the Old Testament, said the angel of the Lord chased his enemies and persecuted them. David's angels fought for his cause and he rejoiced in that fact.

> *"Let them be as chaff before the wind: and let the angel of the LORD chase them. Let their way be dark and slippery: and let the angel of the LORD persecute them"* *(Psalm 35:5-6).*

Peter's Angel Delivers Him from Herod

King Herod decided to step up the persecution of the church in order to gain political advantage. First he ordered the killing of the apostle James by the sword. Then when the people gave him a favorable response he decided to put Peter in prison. The night before Peter was scheduled for trial and probable execution the church gathered together at Mary's house for a prayer meeting.

During this time, Peter lay sleeping bound with chains, a soldier on each side and more outside the door. Then an angel came and shaking Peter until he awakened said, *"Quick! Get up!"* As Peter got up his chains fell off. *"Get ready! Put your sandals on,"* the angel admonished. *"Follow me!"*

As Peter followed the angel all of the locked doors clicked open until Peter found himself safely outside of the prison and in the street. Only then did the angel leave him.

Peter stood there looking around, wondering if he was asleep and having a very vivid dream. He shook himself and finally realized God had delivered him in a very real, tangible way! *"The LORD has delivered me out of the hand of Herod!"* he exclaimed. Knowing that the church was praying he headed for Mary's house.

When he arrived at the gate, Peter knocked. *"Hurry!"* he muttered. He really wasn't sure he was completely safe. *"I wonder how long it is going to take that bunch of soldiers to realize I am gone?"* He chuckled at the thought.

Finally he heard someone coming. "Great! Won't *they* be surprised!" he mused. "Let me in! *Please!*" he called out.

The girl, Rhoda, who had answered the summons, heard Peter's voice and realized it was him. A shot of adrenalin ran through her from head to toe! A smile spread across her face and she began to run—not to the gate to let Peter in—but back into the house to tell the others.

"Rhoda! Is that you? Would you let me in? *Please?*" Peter pleaded. But Rhoda could not hear him. She was in the house taking charge of the prayer meeting.

"Listen, folks!" she cried. "God has answered our prayers! Peter is outside. He is standing at the gate!"

"Rhoda! Stop that babble. What is wrong with you? You know that Peter is in prison. Are you crazy? If you saw anything out there that looked like Peter it was his angel, not him. Now settle down and let's get back to prayer. Peter's trial is tomorrow! "

> *"And they said unto her, Thou art mad. But she constantly affirmed that it was even so. Then said they, It is his angel"* (Acts 12:15).

Peter could hear folks inside and began to feel a little agitated. He knocked again—this time quite insistently and called out, ***"Please! Let me in! It's Peter. Open the gate!"***

An Angel Smites King Herod

It wasn't long until King Herod faced his final destiny in a dramatic fashion as a result of his displaced loyalties and prejudices against the Christians. It happened as he was sitting on his throne giving a speech. When the people heard his words they shouted, "It is the voice of a god and not a man!"

As soon as they said those words and they were accepted as truth by Herod, an angel of the Lord appeared and smote him. He was eaten of worms and died. In that moment the church was avenged of their enemy.

> *"And immediately the angel of the Lord smote him, because he gave not God the glory: and he was eaten of worms, and gave up the ghost" (Acts 12:23).*

The Chariots of God

The number of angels available is so vast that Scripture refers to that number in vague terms. Angels are often referenced along with chariots and horses; this implies they have all of heaven's resources at their fingertips. They are prepared to go to battle at a moment's notice. Their equipment surpasses that of any terrestrial army!

> *"The chariots of God are twenty thousand, even thousands of angels: the Lord is among them, as in Sinai, in the holy place" (Psalm 68:17).*

Angels Minister to Many

- *Angels delivered Lot by force from the destruction of Sodom (Genesis 19:1, 16).*

- *An angel prepared the way for Abraham's servant when he went to find a wife for Isaac (Genesis 24:7, 40).*

- *Angels met Jacob and camped around him on his journey back to his homeland to meet his brother Esau (Genesis 31:55-32:2).*

- *At the end of life Jacob referred to the angel who redeemed him from all evil (Genesis 48:16).*

- *An angel appeared to Moses in the form of a burning bush (Exodus 3:2).*

- *As the Israelites crossed the Red Sea on dry land an angel protected them from the Egyptians by creating light for the Israelites and darkness for the Egyptian army who pursued them (Exodus 14:19-20).*

- *Angels led the way for Moses as He led the children of Israel to the Promised Land (Exodus 23:20-23, 27).*

- *An angel, the captain of the Lord's host, appeared to Joshua to give him instruction concerning the battle of Jericho (Joshua 5:13-15).*

- *An angel appeared to Gideon to give him instruction regarding the battle with the Midianites (Judges 6).*

- *An angel ministered to Elijah when he felt threatened and discouraged by Queen Jezebel (1 Kings 19).*

- *Angels deceived King Ahab by speaking through the false prophets (1 Kings 22:19-20).*

- *Angels delivered the Israelites from the Assyrians (2 Kings 19:35).*

- *Angelic hosts assisted King David (1 Chronicles 11:9).*

- *Angels delivered Shadrach, Meshach, and Abednego from the furnace (Daniel 3:27-28).*

- *Angels shut the lions' mouths when Daniel was thrown into the lions' den (Daniel 6:21-23).*

- *Angels ministered to Daniel when he felt weak and afraid (Daniel 10).*

- *The angel Gabriel appeared to Zacharias regarding the birth of John the Baptist (Luke 1:18-20).*

- *Angels ministered to Jesus during His extended fast (Mark 1:13).*

- *Angels strengthened Jesus in the garden (Luke 22:42-44).*

- *Angels wish they could partake of the salvation plan that we as saints enjoy (1 Corinthians 4:9; 1 Peter 1:11-12).*

- *Angels rejoice whenever someone repents (Luke 15:10).*

- *Angels released the apostles from prison (Acts 5:18-20).*

A most remarkable story—a favorite angel story for many—regarding Elisha, his servant, warrior angels, and chariots of fire is told in the following paragraphs.

The Syrian King Searches for the Traitor

When the Syrian king plotted to destroy Israel, Elisha miraculously knew, understood, and revealed to the king of Israel everything the Syrians planned in their private war council meetings. Perhaps Elisha's angels attended those sessions.

It became obvious to the Syrian king that a leak of information coming directly from the private meetings of the warlords had been transmitted to the opposing army. The actions of their enemy Israelites made that fact exceeding clear. Deciding that one of his warlords must be a traitor, the Syrian king set out to find and destroy that warrior. Somehow the warlords understood the power of the God of Elisha and responded to the king's interrogation, *"Elisha, the prophet that is in Israel, telleth the king of Israel the words that thou speakest in thy bedchamber."*

> *"Therefore the heart of the king of Syria was sore troubled for this thing; and he called his servants, and said unto them, Will ye not shew me which of us is for the king of Israel? And one of his servants said, None, my lord, O king: but Elisha, the prophet that is in Israel, telleth the king of Israel the words that thou speakest in thy bedchamber"* (2 Kings 6:11-12).

The Syrian King Sets Out to Fetch Elisha

The warlords must have been convincing in their explanation because immediately the king sent out horses, chariots, and a great host of warriors with the command to fetch Elisha and bring him to the king. Obviously the king did not comprehend the power of the God of Elisha. He did not know that the God of Israel had a prophet who remained close to God with access to heavenly hosts in sufficient numbers to protect him.

> *"And he said, Go and spy where he is, that I may send and fetch him. And it was told him, saying, Behold, he is in Dothan. Therefore sent he thither horses, and chariots, and a great host: and they came by night, and compassed the city about"* (2 Kings 6:13-14).

Syrian Warriors Circle the City

The warriors arrived at night and circled the city where Elisha lived so that none could come or go without their knowledge. The servant of Elisha looked out early in the morning and seeing the great host of the Syrians he felt afraid.

Elisha looked and instantly comparing them to the heavenly hosts that God assigned to protect him, felt no fear. When the servant came and asked, *"Alas, my master! How shall we do?"* Elisha responded with words of faith and not of fear.

> *"And when the servant of the man of God was risen early, and gone forth, behold, an host compassed the city both with horses and chariots. And his servant said unto him, Alas, my master! how shall we do?"* (2 Kings 6:15)

Elisha Responds to Fear with Faith

Elisha responded to the fear expressed by his servant with comforting words that ring through the ages as God's children face difficulties that appear to be more than we can bear. *"Fear not: for they that be with us are more than they that be with them"* (2 Kings 6:16).

Elisha Prays that the Servant's Eyes Be Opened

Looking toward the surrounding mountains, Elisha saw thousands of God's mighty angels driving chariots of fire. They were ready and willing to fight any battle that needed to be won for God's special prophet, Elisha. Then Elisha prayed that God would open his servant's eyes so he could also see through eyes of faith and comprehend God's delivering power.

> *"And Elisha prayed, and said, LORD, I pray thee, open his eyes, that he may see. And the LORD opened the eyes of the young man; and he saw: and, behold, the mountain was full of horses and chariots of fire round about Elisha"* (2 Kings 6:17).

At Times God Sends Judgment Instead of Mercy

Though God is a God of great mercy, He has set limits. When He sends judgment instead of mercy there is no escape. Angels are aware of this. They understand the judgments of God and are involved in that. However, when God extends mercy, it comes directly from Him. He does not involve the angelic hosts.

> *"Behold, I send an Angel before thee, to keep thee in the way, and to bring thee into the place which I have prepared. Beware of him, and obey his voice, provoke him not; for he will not*

pardon your transgressions: for my name is in him" (Exodus 23:20-21).

He Is Great and Very Terrible

God's judgments are as real as His mercy. Examples of this in Scripture help us to comprehend the greatness and the terribleness of God. The prophet Joel reminds us there are two sides to the almighty God of the universe.

> *"And the LORD shall utter his voice before his army: for his camp is very great: for he is strong that executeth his word: for the day of the LORD is great and very terrible; and who can abide it?" (Joel 2:11).*

Lucifer, a Fallen Angel

Satan, or Lucifer, is a fallen angel. One day he decided he would take the power given to him by God and use it to become equal with or rise above God. God sent swift and certain judgment banishing him from heaven forever.

> *"How art thou fallen from heaven, O Lucifer, son of the morning! how art thou cut down to the ground, which didst weaken the nations! For thou hast said in thine heart, I will ascend into heaven, I will exalt my throne above the stars of God: I will sit also upon the mount of the congregation, in the sides of the north: I will ascend above the heights of the clouds; I will be like the most High. Yet thou shalt be brought*

down to hell, to the sides of the pit" (Isaiah 14:12-15).

Hell Is Prepared for the Devil and His Angels

Hell—a place of eternal judgment and everlasting fire burning forever—was prepared for the devil and his angels, not for mankind; however, those who follow Satan and are deceived by him will fall into the same damnation.

> *"And the King shall answer and say unto them, Verily I say unto you, Inasmuch as ye have done it unto one of the least of these my brethren, ye have done it unto me. Then shall he say also unto them on the left hand, Depart from me, ye cursed, into everlasting fire, prepared for the devil and his angels" (Matthew 25:40-41).*

Evil Angels, Noah, Sodom and Gomorrah

God judged Lucifer's rebellion by casting him and his evil angels out of heaven. He destroyed everyone on the earth at the time of Noah except for Noah and his family. He turned the cities of Sodom and Gomorrah into ashes. These are examples of God's judgments in the earth.

> *"For if God spared not the angels that sinned, but cast them down to hell, and delivered them into chains of darkness, to be reserved unto judgment; and spared not the old world, but saved Noah the eighth person, a preacher of righteousness, bringing in the flood upon the world of the ungodly; and turning the cities of*

> *Sodom and Gomorrha into ashes condemned them with an overthrow, making them an ensample unto those that after should live ungodly. … But these, as natural brute beasts, made to be taken and destroyed, speak evil of the things that they understand not; and shall utterly perish in their own corruption" (2 Peter 2:4-6, 12).*

Satan's Power Is Limited

Satan has limited power on the earth as he tries to get back at God by badgering His saints. If we had any idea how little power he really has we would say with the prophet Isaiah, *"Is this the man that made the earth to tremble?"*

> *"They that see thee shall narrowly look upon thee, and consider thee, saying, Is this the man that made the earth to tremble, that did shake kingdoms; that made the world as a wilderness, and destroyed the cities thereof; that opened not the house of his prisoners?" (Isaiah 14:16-17)*

Angels and the Children of Israel Who Died in the Wilderness

After the Israelites experienced God's mercy during the exodus from Egypt, God pronounced judgment upon those who did not obey and believe; they all died in the wilderness.

> *"For the children of Israel walked forty years in the wilderness, till all the people that were men of war, which came out of Egypt, were*

> *consumed, because they obeyed not the voice of the LORD: unto whom the LORD sware that he would not shew them the land, which the LORD sware unto their fathers that he would give us, a land that floweth with milk and honey" (Joshua 5:6).*

Lucifer and the angels that chose to side with him are doomed to everlasting chains of darkness and judgment.

> *"I will therefore put you in remembrance, though ye once knew this, how that the Lord, having saved the people out of the land of Egypt, afterward destroyed them that believed not. And the angels which kept not their first estate, but left their own habitation, he hath reserved in everlasting chains under darkness unto the judgment of the great day" (Jude 5-6).*

Because of this everlasting judgment and its connection with rebellion and disobedience, angels that fear God stay away from rebellious spirits that would hinder them. We as Christians value a pure heart and hate rebellion of any kind because we want to entertain angels in our lives on a regular basis. When they are entertained by those with pure hearts they respond. The promise of their everyday provision is given to those who fear God and keep His commandments.

> *"The angel of the LORD encampeth round about them that fear him, and delivereth them" (Psalm 34:7).*

Power on Her Head in, by, and through Angels

Grasping the value of submission and its link to angels is monumental. Scripture clearly indicates that what we do with our hair matters.

> *"For a man indeed ought not to cover his head, forasmuch as he is the image and glory of God: but the woman is the glory of the man. ... For this cause ought the woman to have power on her head because of the angels" (1 Corinthians 11:7, 10).*

The Words "Ought," "Power," and "Because"

When Greek scholars break the previous verse down by directly translating some of the words, we find additional information that assists us in understanding its meaning:

- *Ought = to owe or be indebted*

- *Power = ability; authority rule; implies freedom for the community*

- *Ability to perform an act, the right, the authority; the permission conferred by a higher court*

- *Because = through, by, or with*

Author and world-renowned speaker Lee Stoneking offers the following conclusions:

> *For this cause the woman is owing or indebted to the inward power which is conferred upon*

her by a Higher Court with or by the angels. If a woman allows her hair to grow long, uncut, in compliance with God's relationship to man, then the church community has a FREEDOM in the Spirit which does not exist without her compliance (Lee Stoneking, The Order of Creation, audio CD).

Her Compliance Brings Blessings to All

As virtuous women of God submit to spiritual authority over them, the power conveyed to them in, by, and through the angels benefits both them and their leadership. Ultimately, the entire church community is blessed because of a lady's continued compliance with these ordinances.

Angels, Rebellion, and Obedience

When we entertain rebellion, God's angels forsake us because they are commanded to protect and minister only to those that fear God. Rebellion is strongly connected to witchcraft, and the holy angels of God want nothing to do with it.

"For rebellion is as the sin of witchcraft, and stubbornness is as iniquity and idolatry" (1 Samuel 15:23).

Angels know judgment accompanies rebellion. When godly men and women fear God and keep His commandments, angels reside close by. When Christians rebel, angels are released from their responsibility to protect and minister to them; they are commissioned to minister only to those who fear God and keep His commandments.

These powerful motivations—unhindered prayers and power in, by, and through the angels—give any lady of God ample incentive to carefully protect her hair from scissors and to avoid rebellious spirits at all cost.

Rebecca Streety

Points to Ponder

- Satan may have tricked Eve into disobeying God's commands but we can overcome the damage through obedience.
- Lucifer is a fallen angel.
- Evil angels fear God and tremble at His power.
- Satan's power is limited by God.
- When a woman does not cut her hair, her life becomes interactive with angelic forces.
- The number of angels is too many to count—there are multitudes of them.
- Angels execute vengeance on our enemies.
- We are protected by angels.
- The Bible gives us many examples of ministering angels.
- At times God sends judgment instead of mercy. God is great but He is also very terrible.
- Mercy comes directly from God and does not involve angels.
- Hell is prepared for Lucifer and his angels.
- When a woman complies with God's holy ordinance and does not cut her hair, she has power on her head in, by, and through the angels.
- The entire church community is blessed by a woman's continued compliance with God's plan of submission.
- Rebellion is as the sin of witchcraft and the angels of God want nothing to do with rebellion.
- If we want to be continually accompanied by angels we will do all we can to fear God and keep His commandments.

Prayers

- Lord, when you came to earth to offer Yourself as a sacrifice for our sin, You gave us a second chance. I am so grateful!
- Thank You for making a way for us to have dominion power over the enemy.
- I will destroy the influence of Eve's disobedience in my life by following Your simple plan of obedience.
- Jesus, I am a holy woman of God and do not cut my hair. Thank you for providing angelic forces to accompany me and those that I minister to.
- Lord, I am a man and want to thank You for angels that accompany our family and church community because of my connection to holy women of God who do not cut their hair.
- God, when I think of angels and realize that there are more of them than can be counted, I am reminded of Your vast power and greatness! My God is GREAT!
- When I am attacked by enemy forces of any kind, I know that You have promised to send Your angels to fight for me. That is such a relief! YOU FIGHT MY BATTLES! Thank You, Jesus!
- Jesus, as I read through Your Word and think about all of the stories You included to remind us of the angelic forces at work, I am overwhelmed with faith to trust You to take care of me.
- I understand that Lucifer is a fallen angel who works to deceive us. Lord, I want to avoid his deceptive forces at all cost.
- God, I know that even evil angels tremble when they think of Your power and greatness. How much more should I fear You and keep Your commandments. Would You help me in the following areas?
- Jesus, You are all powerful and able to limit any power the enemy has. That is exciting! YOU ARE THE BEST!
- Lord, You are great but also very terrible. I know that You often extend mercy but You also execute judgment. I want no part in Your judgments after life is over but while I am living I will judge myself according to the Bible.
- Jesus, it is exciting to think about having power on my head in, by, and through the angels. I understand this is connected to my submission to authority, as You set it up, and benefits the entire church community.
- God, protect me from rebellious spirits at all cost. I want to attract the holy angels that obey Your commands in answer to my prayers.

Prayer and Hair

- Avoiding Shame and Dishonor
- Hair, Not a Veil or a Hat
- Is It Okay to Trim Our Hair?
- Nature Teaches Us
- The Spirit of Holiness (Includes article by Dr James Hughes)

CHAPTER 8

AVOIDING SHAME AND DISHONOR

"Her Hair Is Given Her for a Covering"

One significant reason to comply with the simple ordinances regarding hair and gender distinction is that failure to do so causes shame and dishonor. Ladies avoid shame and dishonor by going to God with their heads covered—or their hair neither cut nor trimmed. Men avoid shame and dishonor by going to prayer with their heads uncovered—or by the regular clipping of their hair.

> *"But every woman that prayeth or prophesieth with her head uncovered dishonoureth her head: for that is even all one as if she were shaven. For if the woman be not covered, let her also be shorn: but if it be a shame for a woman to be shorn or shaven, let her be covered. For a man indeed ought not to cover his head, forasmuch as he is the image and glory of God: but the woman is the glory of the man" (1 Corinthians 11:5-7).*

Defining Terms

The dictionary meaning of the word "shame" is: *The painful feeling arising from the consciousness of something dishonorable, improper, ridiculous, etc., done by oneself or another: She was overcome with shame* (www.dictionary.com).

There is more than one Greek word that is translated as "shame" in the New Testament. In this case, the word "shame" comes from the word *aischron*, which refers to something that is a disgrace. The root is *aischros*, which is translated as base or filthy.

Vine's Expository Dictionary of the New Testament defines *aischros* as "That which is opposed to modesty or purity."

The Complete Word Study Bible Dictionary says this about the word "shame" in 1 Corinthians 11:6:

> It occurs in 1 Corinthians 11:6, referring to the shame that a woman brings upon herself if she cuts off or shaves her hair, because such was the custom of lewd women, especially the prostitutes serving at the temple of Aphrodite on Corinth. A decent woman always was distinguished by hair which covered the head well, a sign of decorum (etiquette) and propriety (proper).

The meaning of the word "dishonor" is *to deprive of honor; disgrace; bring reproach or shame on.*

The Result of Sin and Shame

Avoiding the painful *feeling* that shame and dishonor impose upon an individual is only one incentive to avoid it. The most significant reason to avoid shame is that it brings damnation to the soul.

> *"Marvel not at this: for the hour is coming, in the which all that are in the graves shall hear his voice, and shall come forth; they that have done good, unto the resurrection of life; and they that have done evil, unto the resurrection of damnation" (John 5:28-29).*

Holiness Pleases God

God delights in the obedience of mankind and their adherence to the simple plans He lays out in His Word.

> *"Follow peace with all men, and holiness, without which no man shall see the Lord" (Hebrews 12:14).*

Cleansing ourselves from sin, shame, and dishonor is a constant job as we monitor each of the sensory gates that allows the senses to function. The body houses five methods of perception, or senses: *hearing, sight, touch, smell, and taste.* When we allow sin to enter into our lives through the gates of our senses, we feel the gentle tug of the Spirit as God convicts us. Often this is preempted by a loss of the feeling of peace that we treasure. As we search His Word and seek to follow His master plan we are once again freed from sin and shame.

> *"Having therefore these promises, dearly beloved, let us cleanse ourselves from all filthiness of the flesh and spirit, perfecting holiness in the fear of God" (2 Corinthians 7:1).*

A Conscience Free from Offense

Working to consistently keep the conscience clear of offense toward God is the privilege of those who love God and keep His commandments.

> *"And herein do I exercise myself, to have always a conscience void of offence toward God, and toward men" (Acts 24:16).*

Ignoring the answer of the conscience as we study the Word to understand the will of God brings shipwreck to our eternal souls.

> *"Holding faith, and a good conscience; which some having put away concerning faith have made shipwreck" (1 Timothy 1:19).*

As we accept the commands regarding submission, hair, and our place in the body of Christ we may be called upon to ignore current trends that openly disregard God's plan.

As Paul closed his argument regarding the hair issue, he asked a question that says in essence, *"After all of the evidence we have presented, judge for yourself: is it a good idea to ignore this simple ordinance?"*

> *"Judge in yourselves: is it comely that a woman pray unto God uncovered?"* (1 Corinthians 11:13)

Fear God and Keep His Commandments

It is our responsibility as Christians to fear God and keep His commandments. To fail to do so is to fall into eternal damnation. It is our desire to avoid this at all cost.

> *"Let us hear the conclusion of the whole matter: Fear God, and keep his commandments: for this is the whole duty of man"* (Ecclesiastes 12:13).

The Fear of the Lord Is the Beginning of Wisdom

The fear of the Lord is foundational for our walk with God.

> *"The fear of the LORD is the beginning of wisdom: a good understanding have all they that do his commandments: his praise endureth for ever"* (Psalm 111:10).

The fear of God does not make us afraid to be in His presence but rather gives us incentive to avoid shame and dishonor at all cost. Godly fear brings an understanding of our place of submission to the God of the universe.

> *"The fear of the LORD is the beginning of wisdom: and the knowledge of the holy is understanding"* (Proverbs 9:10).

He Who Overcomes Inherits All Things

It is exciting to think about eternal life in heaven with the Lord. This is promised to those who overcome sin by the power of the Holy Ghost.

> *"He that overcometh shall inherit all things; and I will be his God, and he shall be my son. But the fearful, and unbelieving, and the abominable, and murderers, and whoremongers, and sorcerers, and idolaters, and all liars, shall have their part in the lake which burneth with fire and brimstone: which is the second death. And there came unto me one of the seven angels which had the seven vials full of the seven last plagues, and talked with me, saying, Come hither, I will shew thee the bride, the Lamb's wife" (Revelation 21:7-9).*

Angels Gather Saints from the Four Winds

When Jesus returns for His church, the angels will blow the trumpet of God. This will make a great sound that resounds through the ages and assists them in gathering the saints of God together.

> *"And he shall send his angels with a great sound of a trumpet, and they shall gather together his elect from the four winds, from one end of heaven to the other" (Matthew 24:31).*

A holy woman of God is willing and excited about complying with the ordinance concerning a lady's long, uncut hair when she considers the consequences of those who disobey the commandments of God and the rewards of those who obey.

> *"Then we which are alive and remain shall be caught up together with them in the clouds, to meet the Lord in the air: and so shall we ever be with the Lord. Wherefore comfort one another with these words" (1 Thessalonians 4:17-18).*

Points to Ponder

- Obeying the simple ordinance regarding our hair helps us to avoid shame and dishonor.
- To please God we must follow holiness.
- Shame is the result of sin and offends the conscience.
- Sin brings eternal damnation.
- Those who fear God and keep His commandments will inherit all things!
- Angels will gather saints of God together from the four winds and take them to heaven to live with Him forever!

Prayers

- I want to fear You, God, and keep Your commandments all the days of my life
- When You send Your angels to gather saints from the four winds of the earth, I want to be in that number! Amen.

My Holy Adornment

 Growing up, I was the girl who trimmed her hair at the first sight of a split end. After being filled with the Holy Ghost, it was difficult for me to imagine not trimming away at those horrid split ends. However, I had a greater concern that overshadowed my concerns about my hair: I was desperate for the presence of God.

 From the first day I entered the church, I wanted the power I felt. It was so different from anything I had experienced before and so real! I was not accustomed to adhering to biblical doctrines of holiness but I did not care. Whatever it took, however difficult, I wanted God and I wanted truth. Little by little God revealed to me the unique privilege and honor I had to submit my life to Him through my uncut hair.

My wonderful pastor and teachers helped me understand the meaning behind it. It is more than a "rule." I saw for myself how Scripture teaches a woman not to cut her hair. It is unarguable.

I gained access to the power I longed for through submission. What an honor that God would choose us to be His sacred vessels! It is not only a duty but an honor to be holy and set apart!

"Give unto the LORD the glory due unto his name; worship the LORD in the beauty of holiness" (Psalm 29:2).

The word "beauty" in this verse can better be translated as, "a holy adornment." I am so thankful that instead of the makeup and other things I used to adorn myself with, the holiness that comes through my uncut hair is now my adornment. After making what I thought at first would be a sacrifice, I now feel more beautiful than ever before.

—*Rachel Thacker*

A Lady's Hair Is Her Glory

Anita Joy Sargeant

*"Today I will spend time lighting a light
and not on cursing the darkness...
There are so many lights that are longing to be lit."*

CHAPTER 9

HAIR, NOT A VEIL OR A HAT

"Her Hair Is Given Her for a Covering"

Powerful, Effective Prayers

Scripture states that a lady's head should be covered when she prays and a man's head should be uncovered. What does that mean? Does it mean that when a man prays he should not wear his hat or that a lady should always wear a veil or hat when she prays?

> *"Every man praying or prophesying, having his head covered, dishonoureth his head. But every woman that prayeth or prophesieth with her head uncovered dishonoureth her head: for that is even all one as if she were shaven"* (1 Corinthians 11:4-5).

Her Hair Is Given Her for a Covering

The answer is revealed just a few verses later. A lady's *hair* is given her for a covering! When a man or a woman cuts their hair, the head is considered "uncovered."

> *"Judge in yourselves: is it comely that a woman pray unto God uncovered? Doth not even nature itself teach you, that, if a man have long hair, it is a shame unto him? But if a woman have long hair, it is a glory to her: for her hair is given her for a covering"* (1 Corinthians 11:13-15).

God linked obedience to this simple ordinance to answered or unanswered prayer. Hair is given by God so that when obedience to this ordinance is followed, prayer can be made at a moment's notice anywhere, anytime. There is no need for a lady to first go and find a suitable hat to cover her head before her prayers are effective. There is no need for a man to take off his hat before God will hear his prayer.

Pray Always

Since Scripture commands that we pray without ceasing—or be constantly in contact with God during our everyday plans and events—the fact that hair is our covering instead of a hat or a veil makes complete sense.

> *"Watch ye therefore, and pray always, that ye may be accounted worthy to escape all these things that shall come to pass, and to stand before the Son of man"* (Luke 21:36).

Points to Ponder

- A lady's head should be covered when she prays.
- A man's head should be uncovered when he prays.
- Hair is the covering, not a hat or a veil.
- A lady's head is covered if she does not cut her hair.
- A man's head is uncovered if he regularly clips his hair.
- Since hair is the covering, we are able to pray effective prayers at any time of the day or night.

Prayers

- Jesus, I am a lady and pledge to cover my head with uncut hair so that my prayers are effective.
- Lord, I am a man and will regularly cut my hair so that my prayers are effective.
- Thank You for this simple plan for effective prayers. I love You, Jesus!

A Lady's Hair Is Her Glory

Shiloh Andrus

CHAPTER 10

IS IT OKAY TO TRIM OUR HAIR?

"Her Hair Is Given Her for a Covering"

It is clear that the Bible commands ladies to have long hair. But just how long is long? If we trim the ends, are we still in obedience?

Shorn? Shaven?

The words "shorn" and "shaven" are both mentioned in the passage in 1 Corinthians on hair. What is the difference between the two words?

> *"For if the woman be not covered, let her also be shorn: but if it be a shame for a woman to be shorn or shaven, let her be covered"* (1 Corinthians 11:6).

According to the dictionary, the word "shorn" comes from the word "shear" and means to *cut or clip the hair*. Shaven comes from the word "shave" and means to *cut the hair off very close to the skin*.

Scripture states it is a shame for a woman to either be shorn *or* shaven. After studying the meaning of these words, we come to the conclusion that a woman should not cut her hair at all.

How Long Is Long?

How does one let the hair grow long? When we look at the word "long" we find that the original Greek word is *keiro*, meaning "uncut" or "untrimmed." The meaning of the word "long" is uncut.

> *"But if a woman have long hair, it is a glory to her: for her hair is given her for a covering"* (1 Corinthians 11:15).

When a woman does not cut her hair, her hair is "long" in God's eyes. She is in obedience to the ordinance given regarding gender distinction and hair.

Will It Grow Faster If I Cut It?

Some are under the impression that the only way for their hair to grow longer is to cut it. While that seems an oxymoron, many women subscribe to this delusion for the following reason: when a woman cuts her hair, the body rapidly works to correct the loss. However, once the hair *returns to its intended length* it then remains at that length indefinitely or until life seasons or health issues change it. Generally a lady's hair is not as long or as thick when she is older than it was when she was in her prime.

Many times ladies trim their hair believing it will grow longer than it would if they did not. Not only is this false, but it is in direct disobedience to Scripture. The Bible clearly teaches that long hair means "uncut."

We Inherit Hair Length Tendencies

Very few ladies who do not cut their hair have hair that grows to reach ankle length; fewer still have hair that grows longer than that. Most ladies have hair that stops growing at either the mid-back or waist.

As in other physical characteristics, hair length is linked to inherited tendencies. Various cultures have different hair tendencies. Just as God never makes two snowflakes exactly alike, no two ladies have identical hair. Hair varies in numerous ways: length, color, straight, curly, thick, thin, fine, course, oily, dry, and so on.

If a woman consistently cuts her hair, she does not know what her inherited hair length is. Only when she allows her hair to grow "long" does she learn what it is.

Accepting God's Authority

While Scripture is clear about this issue, God still leaves the decision up to each individual. Men have the ability to grow their hair long and women can cut their hair. It is important to remember that God's protection will be forfeited by this act of disobedience. If men and women choose, however, to conform to God's authority, He will bless and empower them to do His will.

Points to Ponder

- In order to comply with the ordinance regarding hair a lady should not cut her hair at all.
- The word "long" in 1 Corinthians 11:15 comes from the Greek word "keiro" and means uncut.
- When a woman does not cut her hair, it is long in God's eyes.
- When a woman cuts her hair, it begins to rapidly grow to correct the loss. God uses nature to help her bring it back to its intended length.
- We inherit our hair length tendency.

Prayers

- Jesus, I am a holy woman of God and will not cut my hair at all.
- Thank You for helping me to understand what it means for a woman to have "long" hair. I have worried because my hair is not as long as some of the other sisters and I wondered if You were unhappy with me because of it.
- Lord, I choose to follow Your will and to submit to Your authority in my life.

Shiloh Andrus

A Lady's Hair Is Her Glory

Rachel Thacker

Chapter 11

Nature Teaches Us

"Her Hair Is Given Her for a Covering"

Paul Finishes His Dissertation with a Final Point

Paul concluded his comments concerning submission, hair, and their connection to prayer by making one last significant point. Nature teaches us to allow our hair to grow long if we are ladies and to cut it if we are men.

> *"Doth not even nature itself teach you, that, if a man have long hair, it is a shame unto him? But if a woman have long hair, it is a glory to her: for her hair is given her for a covering"* (1 Corinthians 11:14-15).

In other words, it is not unreasonable for God to insist that men pray with short hair and that ladies allow their hair to grow. Our inbred sense of nature points us in that direction. Though the younger generation may not realize it, the widespread custom of cutting a woman's hair is a relatively new phenomenon.

Nature Is God's Teacher

Dictionary.com states that one of the meanings of the word "nature" is *"Instincts or inherent tendencies directing conduct."* Anytime God asks us to follow a simple ordinance such as this one, His creative plans are made obvious in nature. Nature is one of the ways God reveals His will to us.

Bald Men and Bald Women

Many times when men reach mature years they lose their hair. Though they may wish it were not so, often they barely give it a second thought. They go about their daily routine without shame. Ladies, on the other hand, seldom lose all of their hair as they age; it merely thins and often does not grow as long. Complete loss of hair for a lady often indicates disease; she generally tries to cover her head while recovering from her illness.

When Women Cut Their Hair

Nature teaches this ordinance when a woman cuts her hair and it quickly grows back to the correct length, which is determined by her inherited tendencies. When a man cuts his hair it grows back but not at the same rate of speed as a woman who cuts her hair. In this manner nature again teaches us a lesson.

Men Are Attracted to Long, Flowing Hair

Nature teaches this when men are attracted romantically to a feminine lady with long hair more than they are to a lady whose hair is chopped off. Those who create romantic stories often depict a lady with long hair that is carefully arranged in a becoming manner. Her long, flowing hair plays a part in attracting the attention of her male counterpart.

Points to Ponder

- Even nature or instincts or inherent tendencies directing conduct teach us that a lady's hair should not be cut but a man's hair should be regularly clipped.
  - Many times men completely lose their hair when they reach mature years while a lady's hair merely diminishes.
  - When a woman cuts her hair nature teaches us that it quickly grows back to its intended length.
  - Men are attracted to long, flowing hair.

Prayers

- Jesus, thank You for helping me to understand the way that nature teaches us the principles You teach in Your Word regarding gender distinction and how it affects our hair.

A Lady's Hair Is Her Glory

Rebecca Streety

CHAPTER 12

THE SPIRIT OF HOLINESS

"Her Hair Is Given Her for a Covering"

Holiness is beautiful! Following God's plan for our lives does not bring grief but offers us abundant life in this world and a promise of everlasting life after death. We have every reason to rejoice!

"For this is the love of God, that we keep his commandments: and his commandments are not grievous" (1 John 5:3).

The Law Kills but the Spirit Gives Life

If we just concentrate on the law and do not become involved with the Spirit we may miss out on the joy of living for God. The law kills but the Spirit gives life.

"Who also hath made us able ministers of the new testament; not of the letter, but of the spirit: for the letter killeth, but the spirit giveth life" (2 Corinthians 3:6).

The Joy of Walking in the Spirit

When we walk in the Spirit, we enjoy the protection and guidance that come from submission to His perfect plan. The privileges of walking in the Spirit include joy and rest. We gain access to all of God's power and authority. This includes the innumerable company of angels that accompany Him and camp about those who fear Him. We enjoy many other fringe benefits. Every flower seems to bloom a little brighter, the sky appears a little bluer, the grass seems a little greener, and the songbird's melodies a little sweeter. The joy of living for God and walking in the Spirit surpasses all other joys in life. The comfort and rest of the Holy Ghost as it has its way in our lives is priceless. Many would pay large sums to obtain the freedom from guilt and to find the power, protection, peace, and joy God provides for His people.

> *"But let the righteous be glad; let them rejoice before God: yea, let them exceedingly rejoice"* (Psalm 68:3).

Follow Me As I Follow Christ

The eleventh chapter of 1 Corinthians where the hair issue is addressed begins with Paul reminding the saints in Corinth of the importance of following him as He follows Christ. This was more than just a statement of simple obedience because they felt obligated; it was a reminder of a relationship between Paul and the saints in Corinth based on honor for him and his ministry position. To have a solid foundation, we must first understand our position in the body of

Christ and the authority over us. We need to become comfortable spending time with our authority figures becoming acquainted with them and their ways.

> *"And we beseech you, brethren, to know them which labour among you, and are over you in the Lord, and admonish you; and to esteem them very highly in love for their work's sake. And be at peace among yourselves"* (1 Thessalonians 5:12-13).

The foundation of our relationship with God acknowledges that God is the Lord of our lives. It is easy to repent when we find our rightful place.

- *God, You are holy; I am a sinful person.*
- *I am subject to You, Lord.*
- *My life is dedicated to honoring, praising, worshiping, and serving You so I will repent of my sinful ways.*

A Spirit of Holiness Is a Result of Submission

Living for God is realized by acknowledging, recognizing, and honoring God-given authority. Our obedience is inseparable from our relationship with God. When we love Him and keep His commandments, we align ourselves with His promises and His mercy. When we do not, we expose ourselves to the terrible side of God that brings condemnation and judgment.

"And said, I beseech thee, O LORD God of heaven, the great and terrible God, that keepeth covenant and mercy for them that love him and observe his commandments" (Nehemiah 1:5).

Elements of Honor and Respect

When we honor God's authority in our lives, we look for ways to show our respect. Specific elements of honor and respect include the acceptance of responsibility for the role God assigned us in creation. Many live their lives with a posture that communicates superiority to God rather than inferiority. For example, if a person of high rank deserving great honor enters a room where you are comfortably seated, you do not need to perform anything outrageous to communicate disrespect. Simply assume an attitude of indifference and fail to rise or to acknowledge his presence. The same is true with God. If we ignore His commandments and simply assume an attitude of indifference, we are guilty.

Is the Hair Issue a Heaven or Hell Issue?

After we have looked into all of the details concerning the hair issue, we may still hesitate to adhere to the directives given in Scripture. As a way of excusing ourselves, we may ask the question: *"Is the hair issue a heaven or hell issue?"* When one struggles to adhere to simple directives, it is generally an indication of a deeper issue having to do with the heart. We as apostolic Christians are not on a quest to see how *little* we can do to please God but rather how *much* we can do to please Him. When we ask, *"Is the hair issue a heaven or hell issue?"* it indicates we are willing to do only the minimum.

Dr James Hughes of *Life Choice Ministries* addresses the issue of whether hair is a heaven or hell issue in the following article.

> *Over the last several years, I have been asked the same question over and over. The question seems to consume the thoughts of many people and crosses all age groups. "Is the hair issue a heaven or hell issue?" It seems to be the question that many in the church are asking themselves. It deeply troubles me that this question is so prevalent. After much thought, I feel compelled to answer the question being asked. A casual approach to the question does not reveal the deep hidden meaning. The question does not seek to find a true answer; it simply puts the respondent in a defensive posture so the real question cannot be answered without him or her appearing to be judgmental.*
>
> *"Therefore to him that knoweth to do good, and doeth it not, to him it is sin" (James 4:17).*
>
> *The word "good" in this verse is translated from the word "kalov" and means beautiful, handsome, excellent, eminent, choice, surpassing, precious, useful, suitable, commendable, admirable, beautiful to look*

at, shapely, magnificent. Sin is knowing to do beautiful, good things and not doing them. James has just addressed the power of the tongue to give life or death. He says words used wrongly to hurt or injure will produce sin. Sin will keep me out of heaven.

There is a new movement sweeping America. It started in the art world and has now become part of the music, literature, and architecture worlds. It is called minimalism. In art, minimalism is a school of abstract painting and sculpture that emphasizes extreme simplification of form, as by the use of basic shapes and monochromatic palettes of primary colors, objectivity, and anonymity of style, (also called ABC art, minimal art, reductivism, and rejective art). It makes use of the fewest and barest essentials or elements, as in the arts, literature, or design. In the music world it is a school or mode of contemporary music marked by extreme simplification of rhythms, patterns, and harmonies, prolonged chordal or melodic repetitions, and often with a trance-like effect.

Minimalism may work in art, music, literature, and architecture, but it will destroy all relationships. Relationships cannot be based on minimums. I do not think my wife would be very happy with me if I only invested the minimum amount of time, love, affection, commitment, and acceptance into our marriage. "Honey what is the least amount of my time that you need? or what is the minimum of affection that I need to show?" These questions only spell disaster for any relationship. The value that I place on my marriage or friendships defines how much of me I invest in the relationship. I will never ask for the least amount of me that is necessary to invest if I want the relationship to be healthy and last a lifetime.

"Is the hair issue a heaven or hell issue?" When I ask that question, I am asking for a minimum. Paul said he had espoused us to Christ. Just as minimums do not work in the natural marriage relationship, they will destroy the spiritual marriage relationship as well.

The length of a woman's hair is often one of these heaven or hell issues. In 1 Corinthians 11 Paul begins by requesting that they imitate him as he imitates Christ. He then admonishes them to keep the ordinances or traditions that he had taught them. The family structure is then defined. Christ is head of the man and man is head of the woman. Man being the head of the woman goes back to the curse of the Garden.

> "Unto the woman he said, I will greatly multiply thy sorrow and thy conception; in sorrow thou shalt bring forth children; and thy desire shall be to thy husband, and he shall rule over thee" (Genesis 3:16).

A woman's curse is three part. In child bearing and conception she will have great pain and hardship. Her desire will be to her husband. He will rule over her. The word rule means to submit oneself under the authority of someone else. It speaks of someone being placed under the authority of a commanding officer. It is a voluntary act of submission to her husband or her father.

Her curse was not as severe as Adam's was. Adam's curse affects every day of his life, by the sweat of his face (anger) he would till the soil. He would never escape his curse. If she has no children, part of the curse would not apply, her desire for her husband is her choice as well as her submission to him is her choice. Adam had no choice. Every day Adam would struggle to make a living and survive. A woman's long hair is her public statement of submission to the leadership of her husband or her father.

In the city of Corinth, there was a Temple to the goddess Aphrodite. It sat high upon the hill above Corinth. There were over one thousand female prostitutes who were called *"priestesses"* of Aphrodite at this temple. Each of these females had her hair cut off as a sacrifice to Aphrodite. There are stone reliefs showing this very sacrifice. When ships arrived into the harbor at Corinth, the sailor who made it to the top of the hill first was allowed to pick from any of the priestesses he so chose. Sex was used in worship to the goddess of love, Aphrodite.

When a woman in Corinth cut her hair, it showed that she was still involved in the worship of Aphrodite. It was a common practice of most cultures of that day to cut the hair as a sacrifice to their pagan gods. God warned Israel of following this practice.

> "Ye shall not round the corners of your heads, neither shalt thou mar the corners of thy beard" (Leviticus 19:27).

Adam Clarke says "The hair was much used in divination among the ancients, and for purposes of religious superstition among the Greeks; and particularly about the time of the giving of this law, as this is supposed to have been the era of the Trojan war. We learn from Homer that it was customary for parents to dedicate the hair of their children to some god; which, when they came to manhood, they cut off and consecrated to the deity. Achilles, at the funeral of Patroclus, cut off his golden locks which his father had dedicated to the river god

Sperchius, and threw them into the flood." The custom was followed down through the ages until the time of Paul's writing to the church at Corinth. It appears that some women felt that they should offer the same sacrifice to Christ that they had offered to Aphrodite. Paul says "We have no such custom." In verse 10 of 1 Corinthians 11, Paul points out that a woman's power on her head (which is her long hair) affects worship.

> "For this cause ought the woman to have power on her head because of the angels" (1 Corinthians 11:10).

The Jews believed that angels were always present in worship as ministering spirits. The cutting of her hair would affect the ability of angels to minister to man.

Fifty years ago, the world had the same view about long hair for women as the church. In the first season of the I Love Lucy sitcom, one whole episode is about Lucy wanting to get her hair cut. Ricky emphatically says no, she would look like a man. Hollywood had the same view at one time. The hair issue did not appear until the Women's Movement showed up. Its purpose was to free women from the authority of her husband or her father. Because the world has marketed evil so well, their philosophies and ideas are assumed to be "okay" by many

Christians today. Marriage is no longer sacred. Submission is not necessary. Minimums are all that they are looking for.

I Give All to You, Jesus

When we love Jesus Christ we are not focused on minimums, as described in Dr Hughes's article. We are focused on doing our best to please God in every situation. A minimalistic attitude has no passion for relationship. A society based on minimum requirements in relationships is laced with crime, divorce, and chaos.

When we find in Scripture an "eth" ending on a word it adds depth of meaning because the suffix "eth" means "continues to do so." If we love God and keep His commandments and continue to do so, He will love us and continue to do so. This consistency in relationship fosters passion. Without passion we become passive and complacent.

> *"He that hath my commandments, and keepeth them, he it is that loveth me: and he that loveth me shall be loved of my Father, and I will love him, and will manifest myself to him" (John 14:21).*

Points to Ponder

- Following God's plan for our lives does not bring grief but rather brings joy and peace.
- The law kills but the Spirit gives life.
- It is a privilege to walk in the Spirit.
- The Spirit of holiness is a result of submission.
- Specific elements of honor and respect include the acceptance of responsibility for the role God assigned us in creation.
- The hair issue is a heaven or hell issue.
- We are not interested in doing the minimum amount needed to live for God; but we are interested in pleasing Him in any and every way we can.

Prayers

- Jesus, thank You for asking us to do things we can easily do.
- Your indwelling Spirit gives me reason to want to live life to the fullest.
- Lord, I count it a privilege to be one of Your followers.
- Jesus, I submit to you as I put on the Spirit of holiness. I serve You because I love holiness and want to do everything that is possible to make You happy. I love You!

ANITA SARGEANT

Rebecca Streety

History and *Holiness*

- Hair and History
- Set Apart for God

Chapter 13

Hair and History

"Her Hair Is Given Her for a Covering"

Jewish Custom and Hair

Paul wrote to the church in Corinth in detail concerning the hair issue. Many women were being converted who had traditionally sacrificed their hair on an altar to their heathen gods.

According to *International Standard Bible Encyclopedia*, "Long black tresses were the pride of the Jewish maiden and matron." *New Unger's Bible Dictionary* states that "women always wore their hair long." In most places, Paul did not need to address the hair issue because it was not a problem in the Jewish culture.

Easton's Bible Dictionary makes this comment regarding the custom of the Hebrew people during biblical times:

> *Among the Hebrews the natural distinction between the sexes was preserved by the women*

wearing long uncut hair (Luke 7:38; John 11:2; 1 Corinthians 11:6), while the men preserved theirs as a rule at a moderate length by frequent clipping (Easton's Bible Dictionary).

The Hair Issue in the Corinthian Church

In Corinth, the new converts in the church asked if Jesus required them to sacrifice their hair by cutting it off and placing it on an altar as their heathen gods required. Paul responded by explaining gender distinction, submission, and hair. He then made this statement:

> *"But if a woman have long hair, it is a glory to her: for her hair is given her for a covering. But if any man seem to be contentious, we have no such custom, neither the churches of God" (1 Corinthians 11:15-16).*

In other words, the church of the living God does not have the custom of offering a lady's hair sacrificially on an altar. God has a better plan. A lady's long, uncut hair is her glory! It gives her access to power with God. When she complies, her prayers are not hindered.

The Custom of Hair Sacrificed to Idols in Corinth

The Theological Dictionary reports this concerning the city of Corinth and their custom of sacrificial hair:

In biblical times when you entered Corinth, at the top of the hill was the temple of Diana. The first sailor of the sea to reach the top of the hill was given free access to the whole of the harlot harems of the goddess Diana.

The prostitutes in the temple all had short hair. It had been cut off and given as a sacrifice to the goddess, Diana (The Theological Dictionary of the New Testament by Kittle).

A Picture of the Altar

The *National Geographic* quoted in this chapter shows a picture of the altar where women sacrificed their hair. The following caption accompanies the picture:

This altar was found in the city of Aphrodisias, located in southwest Turkey. The temple of Aphrodite towers behind its blazing altar.

Women entered to sacrifice their hair in annual mourning for the death of Aphrodite's lover Adonis (National Geographic Magazine, June 1972, p. 774).

When Did Women Begin Cutting Their Hair?

The historical significance of hair is profound. We find that there was not an issue about women wearing their hair long for the first five thousand nine hundred years of recorded history. For five thousand nine hundred years women in most every culture generally wore their hair long.

The widespread practice of women cutting their hair began in the United States during the Roaring Twenties. The 1920s was a decade defined by its spirit of frivolity, materialism, immorality, and rebellion. The world had survived World War I but not without paying the price of great societal upheaval.

Most of us have pictures of our ancestors taken before the 1920s that tell the tale concerning when women began to cut their hair.

Florence Bartlett Richey, the author's grandmother, born July 25, 1888, in Iowa is pictured here in 1906 at age eighteen. This look was the norm of that day. Modesty and uncut hair for ladies was the expected societal rule. Any variance to this was an exception and for the most part considered unacceptable. Biblical standards of holiness prevailed.

Florence May Bartlett Richey
(Anita Sargeant's grandmother)
Photo taken in 1906, Age 18

Wikipedia Reports on Bobbed Hair

Wikipedia reports concerning the issue of bobbed hair:

> *Historically, women in the west have usually worn their hair long. Although actresses and a few "advanced" or fashionable women had worn short hair even before World War I, — for example in 1910 the French actress Polaire is described as having "a shock of short, dark hair," a cut she appears to have adopted in the early 1890s — the style was not considered respectable until given impetus by the inconvenience of long hair to girls engaged in war work. Renowned dancer and fashion*

trendsetter Irene Castle introduced her "Castle bob" to a receptive American audience in 1915. Popularized by film stars Colleen Moore and Louise Brooks in the early 1920s, it was then seen as a somewhat shocking statement of independence in young women, as older people were used to seeing girls wearing long dresses and heavy Edwardian-style hair. Hairdressers, whose training was mainly in arranging and curling long hair, were slow to realise that short styles for women had arrived to stay, and so barbers in many cities found lines of women waiting outside their shops, waiting to be shorn of hair that had taken many years to grow.

Although as early as 1922 the fashion correspondent of **The Times** was suggesting that bobbed hair was passé, by the mid 1920s the style (in various versions, often worn with a side-parting, curled or waved, and with the hair at the nape of the neck "shingled" short), was the dominant female hairstyle in the Western world. Close-fitting, bell-shaped hats ("Cloche" hats) had also become very popular, and couldn't be worn with long hair. Well-known bob-wearers were actresses Clara Bow and Joan Crawford, as well as Dutch film star Truus van Aalten.

As the 1930s approached, women started to grow their hair longer, and the sharp lines of the bob were abandoned (Wikipedia, bobbed hair).

Bernice Bobs Her Hair

On May 1, 1920, *The Saturday Evening Post* carried a story called "Bernice Bobs Her Hair" by F. Scott Fitzgerald. His insight and articulation of the inner feelings of those involved bears close scrutiny.

In his story, Fitzgerald spins a tale of two cousins. Bernice, visiting her cousin Marjorie, finds that Marjorie is the object of all the male attention while she herself is socially dull and uninteresting. One night Bernice overhears Marjorie telling her mother how unpopular Bernice is. Her Aunt Josephine responds by encouraging Marjorie to do all she can to help Bernice improve.

Upon overhearing her cousin's remarks, Bernice is crestfallen and considers returning home early from her vacation. The next morning during breakfast she confronts Marjorie, telling her that she heard all of her unkind remarks. Marjorie knows a special event has been planned in honor of the two girls by Mrs Deyo whose pet abomination happens to be bobbed hair. With this in mind Marjorie plans to ruin any chance that Bernice's social skills will improve.

Marjorie begins to implement her evil scheme by seeming to sincerely help Bernice with her clothes, her hair, and her conversation techniques. She talks Bernice into using shocking conversation in order to sound witty and interesting. She tells her to announce to the crowd that she plans to bob her hair. Bernice follows all of Marjorie's instructions including the bold conversation concerning bobbing her hair. She succeeds in gaining the male attention she longs for — *including* turning the head of Marjorie's beau, Warren. This latter development is more than Marjorie bargained for!

Just before the big event at the Deyos' house, Marjorie calls Bernice's bluff concerning her public announcement to bob her hair. The following excerpt from that point in the tale tells the rest of the story.

"That's only a bluff of hers. I should think you'd have realized ... There's a lot of bluffs in the world," continued Marjorie quite pleasantly ...

Bernice saw that Warren's eyes had left a ukulele he had been tinkering with and were fixed on her questioningly ...

Bernice looked round again—she seemed unable to get away from Warren's eyes.

"I like bobbed hair," she said hurriedly, as if he had asked her a question, "and I intend to bob mine."

"When?" demanded Marjorie.

"Any time."

"No time like the present," suggested Roberta.

Otis jumped to his feet.

"Good stuff!" he cried. "We'll have a summer bobbing party. Sevier Hotel barber-shop, I think you said."

In an instant all were on their feet. Bernice's heart throbbed violently.

"What?" she gasped.

Out of the group came Marjorie's voice, very clear and contemptuous.

"Don't worry—she'll back out!"

(As the treachery Marjorie had planned begins to come to fruition, her true feelings of loathing for Bernice surface.)

"Come on, Bernice!" cried Otis, starting toward the door.

Four eyes — Warren's and Marjorie's — stared at her, challenged her, defied her. For another second she wavered wildly.

(Bernice's only purpose for declaring that she planned to bob her hair was to appear witty in order to gain social acceptance as Marjorie had suggested. She never dreamed the end result would be overwhelming peer pressure to *do* just that. As the crowd applies pressure, she realizes that to back out will be to admit she has been living behind a façade.)

"All right," she said swiftly, "I don't care if I do."

An eternity of minutes later, riding down-town through the late afternoon beside Warren, the others following in Roberta's car close behind, Bernice had all the sensations of Marie Antoinette bound for the guillotine in a tumbrel. Vaguely she wondered why she did not cry out that it was all a mistake. It was all she could do to keep from clutching her hair with both hands to protect it from the suddenly hostile world. Yet she did neither. Even the thought of her mother was no deterrent now. This was the test supreme of her sportsmanship; her right to walk unchallenged in the starry heaven of popular girls.

Warren was moodily silent, and when they came to the hotel he drew up at the curb and nodded to Bernice to precede him out. Roberta's car emptied a laughing crowd into the shop, which presented two bold plate-glass windows to the street.

Bernice stood on the curb and looked at the sign, Sevier Barber-Shop. It was a guillotine indeed, and the hangman was the first barber, who, attired in a white coat and smoking a cigarette, leaned nonchalantly against the first chair. He must have heard of her; he must have been waiting all week, smoking eternal cigarettes beside that portentous, too-often-mentioned first chair. Would they blindfold her? No, but they would tie a white cloth round her neck lest any of her blood — nonsense — hair — should get on her clothes.

(The previous insight into both Bernice and Warren's thoughts lets the reader know that Bernice highly valued her long, uncut hair and that she did not want to cut it off. Warren, who had admired her so much in the past, is quickly losing interest in her as she follows through with the bizarre plan.)

"All right, Bernice," said Warren quickly.

With her chin in the air she crossed the sidewalk, pushed open the swinging screen-door, and giving not a glance to the uproarious, riotous row that occupied the waiting bench, went up to the first barber.

"I want you to bob my hair."

The first barber's mouth slid somewhat open. His cigarette dropped to the floor.

"Huh?"

"My hair — bob it!"

Refusing further preliminaries, Bernice took her seat on high. A man in the chair next to her turned on his side and gave her a glance, half lather, half amazement. One barber started and spoiled little Willy Schuneman's monthly haircut. Mr. O'Reilly in the last chair grunted and swore musically in ancient Gaelic as a razor bit into his cheek. Two bootblacks became wide-eyed and rushed for her feet. No, Bernice didn't care for a shine.

Outside a passer-by stopped and stared; a couple joined him; half a dozen small boys' noses sprang into life, flattened against the glass; and snatches of conversation borne on the summer breeze drifted in through the screen-door.

"Lookada long hair on a kid!"

"Where'd yuh get 'at stuff? 'At's a bearded lady he just finished shavin'."

(These responses let the reader know that a lady requesting that her hair be cut off was not a socially accepted, oft requested, or commonly viewed event.)

> *But Bernice saw nothing, heard nothing. Her only living sense told her that this man in the white coat had removed one tortoise-shell comb and then another; that his fingers were fumbling clumsily with unfamiliar hairpins; that this hair, this wonderful hair of hers, was going—she would never again feel its long voluptuous pull as it hung in a dark-brown glory down her back. For a second she was near breaking down, and then the picture before her swam mechanically into her vision—Marjorie's mouth curling in a faint ironic smile as if to say:*
>
> *"Give up and get down! You tried to buck me and I called your bluff. You see you haven't got a prayer."*

(As Marjorie watches her plan to socially ruin her cousin ripen and come to fruition, she exploits her satisfaction in order to rub proverbial salt in the wound she has inflicted. In response, Bernice shuts down her senses and hides behind a feeling of denial, knowing that to do otherwise will be to admit to the crowd that she has been living a lie.)

> *And some last energy rose up in Bernice, for she clinched her hands under the white cloth, and there was a curious narrowing of her eyes*

that Marjorie remarked on to some one long afterward.

Twenty minutes later the barber swung her round to face the mirror, and she flinched at the full extent of the damage that had been wrought. Her hair was not curly, and now it lay in lank lifeless blocks on both sides of her suddenly pale face. It was ugly as sin—she had known it would be ugly as sin. Her face's chief charm had been a Madonna-like simplicity. Now that was gone and she was—well, frightfully mediocre—not stagy; only ridiculous, like a Greenwich Villager who had left her spectacles at home.

As she climbed down from the chair she tried to smile—failed miserably. She saw two of the girls exchange glances; noticed Marjorie's mouth curved in attenuated mockery—and that Warren's eyes were suddenly very cold.

"You see"—her words fell into an awkward pause—"I've done it."

"Yes, you've—done it," admitted Warren.

"Do you like it?"

There was a half-hearted "Sure" from two or three voices, another awkward pause, and then Marjorie turned swiftly and with serpentlike intensity to Warren.

(Once the hair has been cut off, Bernice immediately regrets her decision to follow through with her idle threat to bob her hair. All of the others also realize Bernice has been robbed of her glory. This becomes Marjorie's opportunity to move in and take her place once again at Warren's side.)

"Would you mind running me down to the cleaners?" she asked. "I've simply got to get a dress there before supper. Roberta's driving right home and she can take the others."

Warren stared abstractedly at some infinite speck out the window. Then for an instant his eyes rested coldly on Bernice before they turned to Marjorie.

"Be glad to," he said slowly.

Bernice did not fully realize the outrageous trap that had been set for her until she met her aunt's amazed glance just before dinner.

"Why, Bernice!"

"I've bobbed it, Aunt Josephine."

"Why, child!"

"Do you like it?"

"Why, Ber-nice!"

"I suppose I've shocked you."

"No, but what'll Mrs. Deyo think tomorrow

night? Bernice, you should have waited until after the Deyos' dance — you should have waited if you wanted to do that."

"It was sudden, Aunt Josephine. Anyway, why does it matter to Mrs. Deyo particularly?"

"Why, child," cried Mrs. Harvey, "in her paper on 'The Foibles of the Younger Generation' that she read at the last meeting of the Thursday Club she devoted fifteen minutes to bobbed hair. It's her pet abomination. And the dance is for you and Marjorie!"

"I'm sorry."

"Oh, Bernice, what'll your mother say? She'll think I let you do it."

"I'm sorry."

(Aunt Josephine's reaction helps us comprehend the magnitude of the action of Bernice when she cuts her hair. First she herself is shocked, then she worries about what Mrs Deyo will do and then she mourns over how she will explain this action to Bernice's mother.)

Dinner was an agony. She had made a hasty attempt with a curling-iron, and burned her finger and much hair. She could see that her aunt was both worried and grieved, and her uncle kept saying, "Well, I'll be _____!" over and over in a hurt and faintly hostile tone. And Marjorie sat very quietly, intrenched behind a faint smile, a faintly mocking smile.

(Not only does Aunt Josephine react negatively but Bernice's uncle is *"hurt and faintly hostile."* Marjorie continues to revel in her treachery.)

Somehow she got through the evening. Three boys called; Marjorie disappeared with one of them, and Bernice made a listless unsuccessful attempt to entertain the two others—sighed thankfully as she climbed the stairs to her room at half past ten. What a day!

(Bernice obviously has lost her confidence and popularity with the boys because of her decision to bob her hair.)

When she had undressed for the night the door opened and Marjorie came in.

"Bernice," she said, "I'm awfully sorry about the Deyo dance. I'll give you my word of honor I'd forgotten all about it."

(Marjorie cannot help but throw one last emotional javelin to inflict more pain on her already greatly afflicted cousin. Bernice reacts by pretending to be all right but she does not fool Marjorie.)

"'Sall right," said Bernice shortly. Standing before the mirror she passed her comb slowly through her short hair.

A Lady's Hair Is Her Glory

"I'll take you down-town to-morrow," continued Marjorie, "and the hairdresser'll fix it so you'll look slick. I didn't imagine you'd go through with it. I'm really mighty sorry."

"Oh, 'sall right!"

"Still it's your last night, so I suppose it won't matter much."

Then Bernice winced as Marjorie tossed her own hair over her shoulders and began to twist it slowly into two long blond braids until in her cream-colored negligée she looked like a delicate painting of some Saxon princess. Fascinated, Bernice watched the braids grow. Heavy and luxurious they were, moving under the supple fingers like restive snakes—and to Bernice remained this relic and the curling-iron and a to-morrow full of eyes.

(A plan for revenge begins to form in Bernice's mind as she watches Marjorie brush her own luxurious, long, uncut hair. It seems as though Marjorie is brushing her hair in her cousin's room just to mock and further torment her.

As Bernice ponders the problems she will face as she lives with her decision to bob her hair, she realizes she has no desire to stay, even for one more day. She quickly makes some decisions that will shield her from further hurt with the crowd and will avenge her of her adversary. After a few more coy remarks, Marjorie finally leaves the room …)

But as the door closed something snapped within Bernice. She sprang dynamically to her feet, clinching her hands, then swiftly and noiselessly crossed over to her bed and from underneath it dragged out her suitcase ... The train left at one, and she knew that if she walked down to the Marborough Hotel two blocks away she could easily get a taxicab.

Suddenly she drew in her breath sharply and an expression flashed into her eyes that a practised character reader might have connected vaguely with the set look she had worn in the barber's chair—somehow a development of it. It was quite a new look for Bernice and it carried consequences.

(Once revenge begins to take its course, it goes beyond its intended limits. Not only does Bernice lash out at Marjorie with irreparable results but she also lashes out at Warren.)

She went stealthily to the bureau, picked up an article that lay there, and turning out all the lights stood quietly until her eyes became accustomed to the darkness. Softly she pushed open the door to Marjorie's room. She heard the quiet, even breathing of an untroubled conscience asleep.

She was by the bedside now, very deliberate and calm. She acted swiftly. Bending over she found one of the braids of Marjorie's hair, followed it up with her hand to the point nearest the head, and then holding it a little slack so that the sleeper would feel no pull, she reached down with the shears and severed it. With the pigtail in her hand she held her breath. Marjorie had muttered something in her sleep. Bernice deftly amputated the other braid, paused for an instant, and then flitted swiftly and silently back to her own room.

Down-stairs she opened the big front door, closed it carefully behind her, and feeling oddly happy and exuberant stepped off the porch into the moonlight, swinging her heavy grip like a shopping-bag. After a minute's brisk walk she discovered that her left hand still held the two blond braids. She laughed unexpectedly—had to shut her mouth hard to keep from emitting an absolute peal. She was passing Warren's house now, and on the impulse she set down her baggage, and swinging the braids like pieces of rope flung them at the wooden porch, where they landed with a slight thud. She laughed again, no longer restraining herself.

"Huh!" she giggled wildly. "Scalp the selfish thing!"

Then picking up her suitcase she set off at a half-run down the moonlit street (Saturday Evening Post, May 1, 1920).

This story about Marjorie and Bernice—set during the era when bobbed hair was the talk of the day and an issue all over America—reveals to us the true worth of a lady's long, uncut hair. Though some pretend it does not matter, history helps us to understand the intense emotional and spiritual connection.

Della Sells Her Hair

To further emphasize the changes in our thinking during the past century with regard to a lady's uncut hair, let us look at a portion of the story first published in the year 1906 by a famous short story writer, William Sydney Porter, or more commonly referred to as O. Henry.

In his story, "The Gift of the Magi," O. Henry spins a tale that reveals a young bride and groom who are poverty stricken but madly in love and who desire to please one another at Christmas. Each sells their most treasured possession to buy the other a gift. Della cuts off and sells her beautiful hair in order to buy a platinum fob chain for Jim's watch, and Jim sells his watch to buy expensive jeweled combs for Della's long beautiful hair.

O. Henry tells of Jim and Della's first interaction when Jim arrives home that evening and sees his wife's shorn tresses:

> "Jim, darling," she cried, "don't look at me that way. I had my hair cut off and sold because I couldn't have lived through Christmas without giving you a present. It'll grow out again— you won't mind, will you? I just had to do

it. My hair grows awfully fast. Say 'Merry Christmas!' Jim, and let's be happy. You don't know what a nice—what a beautiful, nice gift I've got for you."

"You've cut off your hair?" asked Jim, laboriously, as if he had not arrived at that patent fact yet even after the hardest mental labor.

"Cut it off and sold it," said Della. "Don't you like me just as well, anyhow? I'm me without my hair, ain't I?"

It is obvious that both Jim and Della would have been much happier simply to spend time together at Christmas. The chain she bought for the watch meant nothing once he no longer had a watch and the combs for her hair were of no use once her hair had been cut off.

The main point is that the loss of her long, uncut hair dealt a blow to both Della and Jim. Though some would like to pretend that hair is just hair and it does not matter, the evidence against such a notion is profound as we study history.

A Moral Issue

Though many ladies today cut their hair simply because it is fashionable or convenient; through the ages short hair on women has signified loose morals and has been linked with pornography. The *Washington City Paper* ran an article by Amanda Hess on August

31, 2009, entitled "The Bob Haircut: Secret Sex Fetish Favored by Prostitutes."

The term *"flapper"* was coined as more and more women began to bob their hair and engage in shocking behavior. The following definition of a *"flapper"* is found on the website www.wikihow.com:

> ***Know what a Flapper girl is.*** *The dictionary defines a flapper as - "A young woman, especially one in the 1920s, who showed disdain for conventional dress and behavior." That is, conventional in the 1920s. The style came around after the first world war, and women were tired of trying to conform to society's idea of normal - women were gaining more independence (e.g. being given the right to vote), and the face of America was changing! Flappers were most commonly known for their dancing, drinking, smoking, wearing a lot of makeup, and a love of films. Almost all flappers had bobbed hair, dated frequently, and stopped wearing their corsets (which were social norms in the 1910s.)*

Is It Just Hair?

During the 1920s no national issue aroused United States citizens more than *"bobbed hair."* Marian Spitzer wrote an article in the June 1925 issue of the *Saturday Evening Post* entitled "The Erstwhile Crowning Glory":

> There hasn't been a newspaper printed in the last two years that hasn't carried some sort of little story about a woman's hair. It used to be a woman's crowning glory, but now it is just hair (Saturday Evening Post, June 1925).

Ann Harding wrote an article in the March 1927 issue of the *Ladies Home Journal* entitled "Your Crowning Glory":

> The most radical change in the costume of women in our times has been the change in hairstyles. Hair really is the crowning glory of a woman. Her hair still remains the most telling item of her appearance and now short hair is considered chic. It is also the symbol of the freedom of women.

There is a price to pay for a nation that refuses to adhere to God's simple instruction regarding gender distinction and submission to authority. This blatant disregard has taken a toll on America during the past century. A study of divorce statistics and crime performed by rebellious youth who were raised in broken homes only begins to tell the tale.

History Supports the Biblical Doctrines on Hair

During the 1960s, rebellion against gender distinction once again raised its ugly head in the form of long hair on men. A significant moral decay occurred as a result of the revolution. The Beatles led the way and soon men everywhere began to exhibit weak and effeminate behaviors; these characteristics hindered their job searches and brought further decay to the family. The term *flower child* was coined as youth congregated in communes, children were born, and often no one knew for sure who fathered the child.

It is noteworthy that nearly all subsequent rebellion in society has been identified with hairstyles. For example, the terms "punk rockers" and "skinheads" are used to refer not only to hairstyles, but to all of the unusual clothing they wear.

History strongly supports the biblical doctrine of long, uncut hair for ladies and regularly clipped hair for men.

In a world that would like us to minimize the importance of long, uncut hair on a lady, feelings such as those described in the stories of Bernice and Della are ignored and scorned as nonexistent. But the honest heart is not surprised at such tales and can relate to them personally.

More important than the historic or moral issues involved are the spiritual implications. History strongly points to the fact that God intended for men to keep their hair trimmed and that women should not cut their hair. Their simple obedience gives them special access to power with God.

Points to Ponder

- Jewish maidens traditionally wore their hair long.
- Some new converts in the Corinth church wondered if Jesus required them to sacrifice their hair on an altar as the heathen gods required.
- Among the Hebrews the natural distinction between the sexes was preserved by the way they wore their hair.
- The widespread practice of women cutting their hair began in the United States during the 1920s after the end of World War I.
- The story "Bernice Bobs Her Hair" carried in the Saturday Evening Post in May 1920 tells the story of the beginning of an era when women cut their hair.
- Though many ladies today cut their hair simply because it is fashionable or convenient, through the ages short hair on women has signified loose morals and is linked with pornography.
- The story of Della and Jim published first in 1906 tells of the value of Della's hair and gives us insight into the changes that have come to our world during the past century.
- During the 1920s no national issue aroused United States citizens more than "bobbed hair." Spitzer wrote in June 1925, "There hasn't been a newspaper printed in the last two years that hasn't carried some sort of little story about a woman's hair."
- History supports the biblical doctrine of long, uncut hair for ladies and regularly clipped hair for men.

Prayers

- Jesus, thank You for making us male and female. I am happy with the way You made me and will do my best to turn the tide in my generation and preserve gender distinction as you commanded in Scripture particularly as it has to do with hair.

ANITA SARGEANT

Woman Kneeling in Prayer
— by Alexandre Couder (French, 1808-1879)
Lord, forgive us as a nation for our sin and heal our land.
My heart is heavy with the sins of your people.

A Lady's Hair Is Her Glory

Rebecca Streety

Chapter 14

Set Apart for God

"Her Hair Is Given Her for a Covering"

A Living Sacrifice

God wants us to *choose* to serve Him. In keeping with His creative purpose, He leaves us a choice in this area. He is a jealous God and desires that we set ourselves apart from the world and follow Him alone.

> *"I beseech you therefore, brethren, by the mercies of God, that ye present your bodies a living sacrifice, holy, acceptable unto God, which is your reasonable service"* (Romans 12:1).

Hair: A Continuing and Incomplete Project

During the creation process, God made many intriguing differences to distinguish male and female; however, He left one thing in our hands to negotiate — our hair. Just as God gave Adam and Eve a choice in the garden, asking them to abstain from only one tree, He gives us a choice and asks us to allow our hair to grow long if we are ladies and to keep our hair cut if we are men. This is something that is continually maintained in order to be effective.

When we adhere to these simple directives concerning our hair, God rewards us with anointed prayers. Anything less than accepting these commands hinders our prayers and causes shame brought on by disobedience.

Evangelist Lee Stoneking states in his message "The Order of Creation":

> *The condition of a man or woman's hair is a continuing and incomplete project, and must be maintained to be accepted by God.*
>
> *A man maintains this relationship by the continued cutting of his hair, while a woman maintains it by the continued growth of her hair. Uncut!* (Lee Stoneking, "Order of Creation," audio CD)

Samson and the Secret of His Power with God

Though God requires that a lady allow her hair to grow long according to the New Testament account in 1 Corinthians, in the Old Testament, we find two instances where God asked men to keep what is known as the Nazarite vow and as a part of that to never cut their hair. One of them was Samuel the prophet and the other was the deliverer named Samson who rose up in the day of the judges. God sent an angel to work out the details of the special agreement with Samson's parents before his birth.

"And the angel of the LORD appeared unto the woman, and said unto her, Behold now, thou art barren, and bearest not: but thou shalt conceive, and bear a son ... and no razor shall come on his head: for the child shall be a Nazarite unto God from the womb: and he shall begin to deliver Israel out of the hand of the Philistines" (Judges 13:3, 5).

Samson accessed phenomenal human strength imparted to him by God as a result of the vow he kept. He used that strength to fight against the Philistines, the arch enemies of the Israelites during that time. As the Spirit of the Lord began to move upon Samson, some of the feats he accomplished single-handedly are enough to boggle the human mind.

- ***A lion attacked Samson and he tore the lion apart.***

    "Then went Samson down, and his father and his mother, to Timnath, and came to the vineyards of Timnath: and, behold, a young lion roared against him. And the spirit of the LORD came mightily upon him, and he rent him as he would have rent a kid, and he had nothing in his hand: but he told not his father or his mother what he had done" (Judges 14:5-6).

- *Samson caught and tied 300 foxes together, set them on fire, and let them loose in a field.*

  "And Samson went and caught three hundred foxes, and took firebrands, and turned tail to tail, and put a firebrand in the midst between two tails. And when he had set the brands on fire, he let them go into the standing corn of the Philistines, and burnt up both the shocks, and also the standing corn, with the vineyards and olives" (Judges 15:4-5).

- *Samson executed his own revenge by single-handedly slaughtering a band of attackers.*

  "And Samson said unto them, Though ye have done this, yet will I be avenged of you, and after that I will cease. And he smote them hip and thigh with a great slaughter: and he went down and dwelt in the top of the rock Etam" (Judges 15:7-8).

- *Samson allowed himself to be tied with ropes and delivered into the hand of the Philistines. Then when they gathered around him, he broke the ropes, took a jawbone of a donkey, and proceeded to kill a thousand of them single-handedly.*

  "And when he came unto Lehi, the Philistines shouted against him: and

the spirit of the LORD came mightily upon him, and the cords that were upon his arms became as flax that was burnt with fire, and his bands loosed from off his hands. And he found a new jawbone of an ass, and put forth his hand, and took it, and slew a thousand men therewith" (Judges 15:14-15).

- **After Samson had killed the thousand Philistines he became very thirsty where there was no water available. He cried out to the Lord and God miraculously provided water for Samson to drink.**

    "And he was sore athirst, and called on the LORD, and said, Thou hast given this great deliverance into the hand of thy servant: and now shall I die for thirst, and fall into the hand of the uncircumcised? But God clave an hollow place that was in the jaw, and there came water thereout; and when he had drunk, his spirit came again, and he revived: wherefore he called the name thereof Enhakkore, which is in Lehi unto this day" (Judges 15:18-19).

For twenty years Samson judged Israel but his unfortunate choices caused an early and tragic end to his deliverance of Israel from the Philistines, and ultimately his life. How much more Samson could have done for God's people if he had continued to honor the vow imposed upon him before his birth!

Samson Gives Away His Secret

There is no middle ground for uncut hair. The story of Samson in the Book of Judges is a powerful example. Samson had always enjoyed the power of the supernatural—a power endued from God Himself and connected to the Nazarite vow that required a man to allow his hair to grow long—uncut. His parents kept the vow as directed by the angel who announced his birth.

Samson's unbelievable human strength felt common and ordinary. He did not know what it felt like to be without that power. For twenty years, God gave him that power to use as he delivered Israel from the hand of the Philistines.

Then the wicked woman Delilah needled Samson until he told her the secret of his strength. Samson did not really believe in the secret of his strength. If he had, Samson never would have revealed the secret to Delilah. He took the power that he had with God for granted, not fearing what would happen if she cut his hair. Possibly he reasoned, *"How could uncut hair be that important?"*

> *"And it came to pass, when she pressed him daily with her words, and urged him, so that his soul was vexed unto death; that he told her all his heart, and said unto her, There hath not come a razor upon mine head; for I have been a Nazarite unto God from my mother's womb: if I be shaven, then my strength will go from me,*

and I shall become weak, and be like any other man" (Judges 16:16-17).

Samson Expected Power without Commitment

Before telling Delilah the truth Samson told her several lies. She responded to his lies by challenging his strength. Surely he knew that if he told her the truth she would cut his hair! After he told her his heart and she cut his hair, she called the Philistines to fall upon him. Samson rose up as at other times and expected the power of God to again be manifested through him but his strength had vanished.

> *"And when Delilah saw that he had told her all his heart, she sent and called for the lords of the Philistines, saying, Come up this once, for he hath shewed me all his heart. Then the lords of the Philistines came up unto her, and brought money in their hand. And she made him sleep upon her knees; and she called for a man, and she caused him to shave off the seven locks of his head; and she began to afflict him, and his strength went from him. And she said, The Philistines be upon thee, Samson. And he awoke out of his sleep, and said, I will go out as at other times before, and shake myself. And he wist not that the LORD was departed from him" (Judges 16:18-20).*

The Tragedy of a Life without Commitment

The Philistines overcame Samson and took advantage of his weakness. They put out his eyes, bound him with fetters, and made him work, doing hard manual labor in the prison house.

> *"But the Philistines took him, and put out his eyes, and brought him down to Gaza, and bound him with fetters of brass; and he did grind in the prison house" (Judges 16:21).*

If we take the power of God lightly in our lives and do not commit to following His commandments, we find ourselves in a place of tragedy. We, like Samson, will be without God's mighty power. The tragedy of a life lived without commitment is a life that is void of divine power.

Samson Repents and His Strength Returns

While Samson spent time grinding in the prison, his hair began to grow. The Philistines did not reckon with God's merciful kindness to Samson. Slowly, God allowed Samson's strength to return as his uncut hair grew long. If the Philistines had really understood the secret of Samson's strength, they would have kept his hair short. Samson's repentance for his folly gave him power once again to fight the Philistines.

> *"Howbeit the hair of his head began to grow again after he was shaven" (Judges 16:22).*

Samson's Revenge and Death

The Philistines called for Samson to be brought out of the prison house and into the arena so they could make fun of him during their celebration. At Samson's request, a boy led him to the main pillars of the house where they had gathered.

> *"Then the lords of the Philistines gathered them together for to offer a great sacrifice unto Dagon their god, and to rejoice: for they said, Our god hath delivered Samson our enemy into our hand. ... And it came to pass, when their hearts were merry, that they said, Call for Samson, that he may make us sport. And they called for Samson out of the prison house; and he made them sport: and they set him between the pillars. And Samson said unto the lad that held him by the hand, Suffer me that I may feel the pillars whereupon the house standeth, that I may lean upon them"* (Judges 16:23, 25-26).

After Samson had taken hold of the main pillars of the house, he bowed his head and began to pray. He asked God for strength to avenge him of his adversaries. As the Philistines laughed at him and scorned the loss of his eyes and his strength, Samson repented and requested that God use him *one more time*.

> *"Now the house was full of men and women; and all the lords of the Philistines were there;*

> *and there were upon the roof about three thousand men and women, that beheld while Samson made sport. And Samson called unto the LORD, and said, O Lord God, remember me, I pray thee, and strengthen me, I pray thee, only this once, O God, that I may be at once avenged of the Philistines for my two eyes"* (Judges 16:27-28).

God heard Samson's prayer. Supernatural strength began to return to Samson and flow through his body as he grasped the pillars and pulled on them with all his might. The massive temple fell and killed all that were present. Samson destroyed more of Israel's enemies at the time of his death than at any other time.

> *"And Samson took hold of the two middle pillars upon which the house stood, and on which it was borne up, of the one with his right hand, and of the other with his left. And Samson said, Let me die with the Philistines. And he bowed himself with all his might; and the house fell upon the lords, and upon all the people that were therein. So the dead which he slew at his death were more than they which he slew in his life"* (Judges 16:29-30).

Totally Committed

The reason God chose hair as a symbol of submission and obedience may be because it takes total commitment to have uncut hair. A person cannot have cut hair one day and uncut the next. It takes time, commitment, and consistency in order to maintain uncut hair. That consistency and commitment is so powerful that it attracts the attention of angelic hosts.

The continual commitment and submission to this ordinance of God is the same commitment and submission that a husband longs for. There is no middle ground of somewhat submitted or somewhat committed. God is a jealous God. He wants to be the one and only. He longs for our complete allegiance much as a groom desires the complete loyalty of his bride.

No groom would be happy if his bride committed to him Sunday through Friday, but on Saturdays she went out and did what she wanted. Even taking one week off each year would be unthinkable. Just as a woman's uncut hair is constant, so is our commitment to the spiritual authority over us. In the right setting that commitment makes us feel safe and secure.

When we separate ourselves unto God, He receives us as sons and daughters. We become fit for the Master's use and His power and authority become our own. He is our Father!

> *"Wherefore come out from among them, and be ye separate, saith the Lord, and touch not the unclean thing; and I will receive you, and will be a Father unto you, and ye shall be my sons and daughters, saith the Lord Almighty"* (2 Corinthians 6:17-18).

Points to Ponder

- God expects us to present ourselves as a living sacrifice. This is our reasonable service to Him.
- The choice to follow the commandments of God regarding our hair is a continuing project for as long as we live.
- During the creation process, God made many intriguing differences to distinguish male and female, but He left one thing in our hands to negotiate—our hair.
- There is no middle ground for cut or uncut hair. It is either one or the other.
- Samson did not value the power of God that he accessed by adhering to the command of God regarding his hair and he gave away the secret of his strength to his enemies.
- Samson's enemies destroyed Samson, leaving him blind and doomed to a life of imprisonment.
- The tragedy of a life lived without commitment is lack of the power of God.
- Samson repented, his strength returned, and as he died he executed vengeance upon his enemies.
- It may be that the reason God chose hair as a symbol of commitment and obedience is because it takes total commitment to have uncut hair.
- God expects total commitment from us much as a groom expects total commitment from his bride.

Prayers

- Jesus, I present myself to You as a living sacrifice. I will keep Your commandments.
- I understand that the hair issue is a continuing project and I pledge to follow Your will as long as I live.
- Lord, I value the secret of my power with You and will not give in to the enemy as Samson did.
- Jesus, I repent of any wrongdoing in the past and ask You to restore the power of God in my life.
- God, I am totally committed to You alone! You are the LORD of my life!
- I LOVE YOU!

Rebecca Streety